THE NATURE OF METAPHYSICS

THE NATURE OF METAPHYSICS

EDITED BY

D. F. PEARS
Fellow of Corpus Christi College
Oxford

LONDON
MACMILLAN & CO LTD
NEW YORK · ST MARTIN'S PRESS
1957

MACMILLAN AND COMPANY LIMITED
London Bombay Calcutta Madras Melbourne

THE MACMILLAN COMPANY OF CANADA LIMITED
Toronto

ST MARTIN'S PRESS INC
New York

PRINTED IN GREAT BRITAIN

CONTENTS

*The essays in this book originated as talks
in the Third Programme
of the B.B.C.*

METAPHYSICS

WE are to enquire what metaphysics is, what distinguishes metaphysics from the rest of philosophy. It seems likely that the question is one which it is particularly difficult to answer neutrally, dispassionately. Many people think that the essential task of philosophers is to provide metaphysical doctrines; some even say that this is the only justification for the existence of philosophers. But many people, including many philosophers, think that all metaphysical doctrines are spurious; some have even called them meaningless. Metaphysics has a unique power to attract or repel, to encourage an uncritical enthusiasm on the one hand, an impatient condemnation on the other. All the more reason for giving, if possible, a neutral and dispassionate account.

The name of the subject is the name given to a treatise by Aristotle. And Aristotle described the subject of his treatise as the science of Being as such, a supremely general study of existence or reality, distinct from any of the special sciences and more fundamental than they. He argued that there must be such a science; since each of the special sciences, besides having its own peculiar subject matter, made use in common with all the others of certain quite general notions, such as those of identity and difference, unity and plurality. Such common notions as these would provide the topics of the general science of being, while various different kinds of existence or reality, each with its own peculiar features provided the subject matter of the more departmental studies.

The conception of metaphysics as a supremely general study which is somehow presupposed by the special sciences, is a fairly enduring one. We find it, for example, though with variations, in Descartes, Leibniz and Kant. But some metaphysicians could have agreed with Aristotle about the comprehensive and general and ultimate nature of their subject without sharing Kant's or Descartes' concern with the foundations of science. Bradley is an example. He says : 'We may agree, perhaps, to understand by metaphysics an attempt to know reality as against mere appearance, or the study of first principles or ultimate truths, or again the effort to comprehend the universe, not simply piecemeal or by fragments, but somehow as a whole'. This agrees with Aristotle in contrasting metaphysics with departmental or, as Bradley would say, fragmentary studies. The 'attempt to know reality' sounds something like 'the study of being as such'. And both would agree on the task of discovering 'first principles'. But Bradley would have ridiculed the idea that he was concerned to get at the presuppositions or foundations of science.

Some contemporary accounts of metaphysics sound, on the face of it at least, very different from either of these. Consider, for example, John Wisdom's description of a metaphysical statement. He says that a metaphysical proposition is, characteristically, a sort of illuminating falsehood, a pointed paradox, which uses language in a disturbing and even shocking way in order to make us aware of hidden differences and resemblances in things — differences and resemblances hidden by our ordinary ways of talking. Of course Wisdom does not claim this to be a complete characterisation, nor perhaps a literally correct one. Perhaps it should itself be seen as an illuminating paradox. In any case, its relation to Aristotle's, or Bradley's, account of the matter is not obvious.

But perhaps a relation can be established. Certainly not all metaphysical statements are paradoxes serving to call attention to usually unnoticed differences and resemblances. For many metaphysical statements are so obscure that it takes long training before their meaning can be grasped, whereas a paradox must operate with familiar concepts; for the essence of a paradox is that it administers a shock, and you cannot shock people when they are standing on such unfamiliar ground that they have no particular expectations. Nevertheless there is a connection between metaphysics and Wisdom's kind of paradox. Suppose we consider the paradox that everyone is really always alone. Considered by itself, it is no more than an epigram — rather a flat one — about the human condition. It might be said, at least, to minimise the differences between being by oneself and being with other people. But now consider it, not simply by itself, but surrounded and supported by a certain kind of argument: by argument to the effect that what passes for knowledge of each other's mental processes is, at best, unverifiable conjecture, since the mind and the body are totally distinct things, and the working of the mind is always withdrawn behind the screen of its bodily manifestations. When the solitude-affirming paradox is seen in the context of a general theory about minds and bodies and the possibilities and limits of knowledge, when it is seen as embodying such a theory, then indeed it is clearly a metaphysical statement. But the fact that the statement is most clearly seen as metaphysical in such a setting does not mean that there is no metaphysics at all in it when it is deprived of the setting. 'Everyone is *really* alone' invites us to change, for a moment at least and in one respect, our ordinary way of looking at things, and hints that the changed view we get is the truer, the profounder, view. And part of Bradley's characterization of metaphysics — 'the attempt to know reality as against mere appearance' — seems to herald a general invitation to a general change of view, which will also be a change to a profounder view. We may surmise, perhaps, that the attempt to secure that comprehensiveness, which both Aristotle and Bradley find characteristic of their enquiry, leads often enough to those shifts of view, expressible in paradox, which Wisdom finds characteristically metaphysical.

But what exactly is the meaning of the requirement that metaphysics should yield a comprehensive system of reality? A theory about the nature of reality might be held to be comprehensive in so far as there were no elements of reality to which the theory did not apply; and might be held to be systematic if the propositions comprised in the theory were interdependent; that is to say, if the propositions of the theory were not divided into a number of independent groups. An extreme case of something systematic in the required sense would be a deductive system in which from a limited number of axioms one could derive, as logical consequences, the remaining propositions of the theory; and it is notable that some seventeenth-century rationalist metaphysicians thought of metaphysics as constituting a deductive system. It might be objected that if we are to understand in this way the idea of a comprehensive and systematic account of reality, then science as a whole, or even some particular science, would qualify as metaphysics; for example, physics, which is certainly systematic enough, might be said to deal with the whole of reality. But this objection has little force. For though physics might be said to be concerned with the whole of reality, it could not be said to be concerned with every aspect or feature of reality. Physical laws may govern, for example, part of the behaviour of living bodies; but if we wish to know about the way organisms develop, we have to go, not to the physicist, but to the biologist. So we can still regard physics as insufficiently comprehensive to qualify as metaphysics. And though science as a whole might be thought to be comprehensive, in that every aspect of reality falls under some particular science or other, nevertheless particular sciences are too independent of one another for science as a whole to count as a single system.

Nevertheless a difficulty remains in drawing a distinction between metaphysics and science. It is perhaps not inconceivable that the sciences might advance to a point at which it would be possible to recast the whole of science as a single system. For example, after enormous strides within biology itself, it might perhaps become possible to reinterpret the basic concepts of biology in terms of the concepts of physics, and so represent biological phenomena as obeying laws which were only special cases of physical laws. What is here envisaged is, roughly speaking, a very large-scale version of the unification effected by the Kinetic Theory of Gases, which brought certain seemingly independent laws concerning gases within a single wider system, by exhibiting them as special cases of dynamical laws. This result was achieved, roughly, by thinking of gases as being composed of particles, and redefining, in terms of the properties of the particles, certain concepts involved in the laws about gases. Such a unification and systematization of the whole of science is of course, at present, the wildest of dreams, and may even be logically impossible, though it has not been shown to be so. But suppose it were to occur; one would still surely refuse to call the resulting systematized science, or even the most general part of it, a metaphysical system.

This refusal would not be the result of mere prejudice. Just because the universal systematized science *was* science, it would not be metaphysics. For even the most general and basic laws it contained would ultimately depend for their acceptability upon the results of observation and experiment in a way which is quite uncharacteristic of the principles of a metaphysical system. The *methods* of science, the tests for acceptability of scientific laws, remain quite different from the methods of metaphysics and the test for acceptability of metaphysical principles. So we have here a further question. For even though it is true that the most general laws or axioms of a unified science would not count as metaphysics, it is also true that many metaphysicians have thought it at least a part of their task to lay, or to lay bare, the foundations of science. We must ask, then, how we are to conceive, or how *they* conceived, of the relations between the metaphysical foundations and the scientific superstructure. That relation, it is clear, is not to be understood simply as the relation of the most general to less general laws of nature.

Many metaphysicians did not explicitly ask themselves this question, nor is it clear what answer they would have given if they had. But there are exceptions. One of them is Kant. He thought there were certain principles which had a quite special place in knowledge, in that they stated the conditions under which alone scientific knowledge of nature, considered as a spatio-temporal system, was possible. These principles were not themselves a part of science. Rather, they embodied the conditions of the possibility of science, and of ordinary everyday knowledge too, for that matter. It was an important part of the metaphysician's task to discover what fundamental ideas these principles involved, and what the principles themselves were; and also to *prove* that they had this peculiar character. For this was the only kind of proof of which they were susceptible. Whatever the shortcomings of Kant's doctrine, it at least gives a clear meaning to saying that metaphysics is concerned with the presuppositions of science, and not merely its most general part.

Yet the shortcomings were important. Kant's fundamental principles varied greatly in character; and very few would now agree that they embodied general presuppositions of the possibility of scientific knowledge. And most would now be very sceptical of the possibility of establishing any rival set of principles with just this status. A more acceptable notion might be that of a body of ideas or principles which were, in something like Kant's sense, the presuppositions, not of scientific knowledge in general, but of a particular *kind* of scientific enquiry, or of the science of a particular time. And this was in fact Collingwood's idea of the nature of metaphysics: the metaphysician exposed the presuppositions of the science of a particular epoch. Only we need not, like Collingwood, think of the metaphysician just as an archaeologist of thought. He might also be, as he has often intended to be and sometimes has been, a revolutionary, fostering new directions in scientific discovery rather than uncovering the foundations of scientific remains.

This line of thought about metaphysics is not peculiar to a relatively traditional thinker like Collingwood. There is at least some analogy between his views and those, for example, of Carnap, who was once a member of the philosophically radical Vienna Circle. Carnap draws a sharp distinction between questions which arise *within* a given system of concepts, or framework of ideas, and questions which are sometimes raised *about* that framework or system. Questions of the first sort belong to the field of some science or of everyday life, and are answered by the methods appropriate to those fields. Questions of the latter sort have traditionally appeared in metaphysics in the misleading form of questions about the reality or existence of some very general class of entities corresponding to the fundamental ideas of the system of concepts in question. Thus philosophers have asked whether there really existed such things as numbers, whether the space-time points of physics were real, and so on. But such questions can be significantly understood only as raising the *practical* issue of whether or not to embrace and use a given conceptual scheme or framework of ideas. To answer affirmatively, according to Carnap, is simply to adopt such a framework for use, and hence to give shape or direction to a whole field of enquiry.

Carnap's view of the matter might seem to make it mysterious that there should be such things as metaphysical assertions, as opposed to metaphysical decisions. The mystery could be solved in principle by regarding metaphysicians as engaged in a kind of propaganda on behalf of some conceptual scheme, the acceptance of which is obscurely felt to be a presupposition of the development of science in a particular direction. Like all forms of propaganda, conceptual or metaphysical propaganda is liable to involve distortion and exaggeration. As Carnap's remarks suggest, one form which conceptual advocacy is liable to take is the entering of a strong claim for the status of *reality* on behalf of some general class of entities, together with a disposition to deny this status to other, less favoured things. At least from Aristotle's time till the end of the eighteenth century, the traditional honorific title for things declared to be real, or ultimately real, was that of *substance*. So we constantly find the entities favoured in any particular metaphysical system being accorded the rank of substances, while everything else is given some inferior, dependent status, or is even declared to be merely appearance. The types of entity favoured in this way have varied enormously. For Berkeley, it was minds or spirits; for Leibniz, some curious mind-like centres of conscious or unconscious experience. Hume was inclined to scoff at the whole notion; but in so far as anything deserved the title, he thought it was individual sense-impressions and images. For Spinoza, on the other hand, it was nothing less than everything: the single comprehensive system of reality, which he called God or Nature.

But the best example for the immediate purpose is provided by Descartes. He, unlike Berkeley and Hume, was a very scientifically-minded philosopher, with very clear ideas about the proper direction for science. He seems to have thought that mathematics, and in particular geometry, provided the model for scientific procedure. And this determined his thinking in two ways. First, he thought that the fundamental method in science was the deductive method of geometry, and this he conceived of as rigorous reasoning from self-evident axioms. Second, he thought that the subject-matter of all the physical sciences, from mechanics to medicine, must be fundamentally the same as the subject-matter of geometry. The only characteristics that the objects studied by geometry possessed were spatial characteristics. So from the point of view of science in general, the only important features of things in the physical world were also their spatial characteristics. Physical science in general was a kind of dynamic geometry. Here we have an exclusive preference for a certain type of scientific method, and a certain type of scientific explanation : the method is deductive, the type of explanation mechanical. These beliefs about the right way to do science are exactly reflected in Descartes' ontology, in his doctrine, that is, about what really exists. Apart from God, the divine substance, he recognized just two kinds of substance, two types of real entity. First, there was material substance, or matter ; and the belief that the only scientifically important characteristics of things in the physical world were their spatial characteristics goes over, in the language of metaphysics, into the doctrine that these are their only *real* characteristics. Second, Descartes recognized minds, or mental substances, of which the essential characteristic was thinking ; and thinking itself, in its pure form at least, was conceived of as simply the intuitive grasping of self-evident axioms and their deductive consequences. These restrictive doctrines about reality and knowledge naturally called for adjustments elsewhere in our ordinary scheme of things. With the help of the divine substance, these were duly provided.

It is not always obvious that the metaphysician's scheme involves this kind of ontological preference, this tendency, that is, to promote one or two categories of entity to the rank of the real, or of the ultimately real, to the exclusion of others. Kant, as much concerned as Descartes with the foundations of science, seems, in a sense, to show no such preference. He seems prepared to accord reality to all the general types of phenomena which we encounter in experience or, rather, to draw the distinction between the illusory and the real, as we normally do, within these types and not between them. Yet it is only a relative reality or, as he said, an empirical reality, that he was willing to grant in this liberal way to all the general classes of things we encounter. For the whole world of nature, studied by science, was declared by him to be ultimately only appearance, in contrast with the transcendent and unknowable reality which lay behind it. So, in a sense, he downgraded the whole of what we know in favour of what we do not and cannot know. But this thoroughgoing contrast between appearance and reality was perhaps of less importance to him in connection with science than in connection with morality. The transcendent reality was of interest to us, not as scientific enquirers, but as moral beings, not as creatures faced with problems of knowledge, but as creatures faced with problems of conduct. Kant was a very ambitious metaphysician, who sought to secure, at one stroke, the foundations of science *and* the foundations of morality.

The last point is of importance. Though a concern with the foundations of science is, or has been, one impetus to the construction of metaphysical systems, it is only one among others. Concern with morality, with the right way to behave, has been scarcely less important. And other disciplines have contributed to the metaphysical drive. In the nineteenth century, for example, when history came of age and began to preoccupy philosophers as science had done in the seventeenth century, metaphysical systems started to grow out of historical studies. Thus the historically minded metaphysician searches for the true nature of historical explanation and concludes, perhaps, that the key concept is that of a certain mode of development of human institutions. Suppose he then extends this theory beyond the confines of history, maintaining that this same concept, which is, in a certain sense, a concept of mental development, provides the only true explanation of the whole universe. The result is a comprehensive system something like Hegel's. Hegel honoured one type of historical explanation by making it the foundation of his system; and it was this system that Marx turned upside down, making the whole process of development material instead of mental.

Systems like those of Marx and Hegel had, and were intended to have, implications regarding human behaviour. But concern with moral and emotional, even with aesthetic, requirements may take many different forms. It may take the form of a desire to provide some transcendental authority, some more than human backing, for a particular morality: moral conclusions about how we ought to behave are to follow from metaphysical premises about the nature of reality. It may take the more general form of a wish to supply transcendental backing for morality in general. Or it may take the form of a wish to demonstrate that there is some surpassing and unobvious excellence about the nature of things, an ultimate satisfactoriness in the universe. Spinoza provides another example of the first of these. He claims to demonstrate, from the nature of reality, that the supreme satisfaction is also the supreme virtue, and that both consist of what he calls the intellectual love of God : which seems to mean, for him, a kind of acquiescent and admiring understanding of the workings of Nature. Kant is the supreme example of the second. The whole world of nature, including our ordinary human selves — the whole province of scientific knowledge, in fact — is declared to be mere appearance, in contrast with the world of transcendent reality, the world of things in themselves. Reality is set behind a curtain impenetrable to scientific enquiry, a removal which both guarantees its security and heightens its prestige. But communications are not wholly severed. From behind the curtain Reality speaks — giving us, indeed, not information, but commands, moral imperatives. In some admittedly unintelligible way, Reality is within us, as rational beings ; and, with unquestionable authority, it lays down the general form of the moral law which we ought, as ordinary human beings, to obey. Finally, Leibniz, who unites so many intellectual concerns in a brilliant, if precarious, harmony, provides a good example of the third form which this element in metaphysics may take. The celebrated optimism — 'Everything is for the best in the best of all possible worlds' — is not, in the context of his system, at all as absurd as Voltaire made out. We may find it unsympathetic, which is another matter ; for Leibniz's criteria of the highest excellence were peculiarly his own. He thought he could demonstrate that reality must exhibit a peculiarly satisfying combination of the maximum possible diversity and richness of phenomena, together with the greatest possible simplicity of natural laws. Sometimes the demonstration appears to be theological, sometimes purely logical. In any case it was this combination of richness and elegance which he found so admirable — worth, no doubt, a Lisbon earthquake or a Turkish war. It seems a taste that we might find unsympathetic, but could scarcely find ridiculous.

It is time, however, to enter a caveat. It would be misleading to suggest that the sources of metaphysics are always of the kinds we have so far described — such as the wish to get morality transcendentally underwritten, or the desire to give science the right direction, or the urge to show that some departmental study holds the key to the universe at large. Metaphysics may have a humbler origin. It often enough happens that philosophers, reflecting upon a particular matter, find themselves, or seem to find themselves, in a certain kind of quandary. We can best illustrate this by considering in a little detail one particular quandary of this kind. We select the problem of our knowledge of the material world, a problem — or apparent problem — which has long occupied the attention of philosophers. On the one hand, in their unphilosophical moments, they (like all the rest of us) have no hesitation in sometimes claiming to know on the evidence of the senses that this or that material object exists or is of such and such a character; they do, in practice, seem to have no difficulty (in many cases) in distinguishing between situations in which it is in order to claim to know, for example, that the milk is on the doorstep and situations in which such a claim would not be in order. Naturally, therefore, they have a strong antipathy to any suggestion that all such claims to knowledge should be rejected as false. Nevertheless, on reflection, they find themselves faced with philosophical considerations which seem to force them into just such a rejection. For (the argument runs) if we are to have perceptual knowledge of the material world, this knowledge must be based on the appearances which material things present to us, on our sense-impressions. But it is clear that our sense-impressions may be deceptive or even hallucinatory; the fact that it looks to me as if there were milk bottles on the doorstep does not guarantee that there really are milk bottles on the doorstep, or even that there is in fact *any*thing on the doorstep. If we try to remove this doubt in a given case by further observation, all we are doing is providing ourselves with further sense-impressions, each of which is open to the same suspicion of deceptiveness as the sense-impressions with which we started; so we are no better off. Indeed (the argument may continue) so far from providing us with certain knowledge about the material world, our sense-impressions cannot even be justifiably regarded as more or less reliable clues to, or indications of, the character of the material world. For they could only properly function as clues if we could correlate particular kinds of sense-impression with particular kinds of material object, and to do this we should have to possess some kind of direct access to material objects, and not merely indirect access via sense-impressions.

This direct access we do not have. This is an example of the kind of philosophical consideration which seems to lead to the conclusion that all claims to knowledge of the material world must be rejected. The result is a quandary of just the kind we are seeking to illustrate : that is to say, a conflict between a reluctance to discard some range of propositions with which in everyday life everyone is perfectly satisfied, and the pressure of a philosophical argument which seemingly leaves no alternative but to reject the propositions in question. The propositions in jeopardy often (though not always) state that we have knowledge of this or that kind, in which case the philosophical arguments which undermine them do so by setting up a barrier between appearance and reality, or between the evidence and that for which it is (supposedly) evidence.

Now, when is the response to such a quandary a metaphysical response? One kind of response, which would be generally admitted to be metaphysical is what one might call the Transcendentalist response. To respond in this way to the quandary about the material world, for example, would be to maintain that material objects may be known to exist, even though not observable, and to explain the possibility of such knowledge by invoking some transcendental hypothesis, some principle which is supposed to be acceptable independently of experience. For example, one might invoke the principle that God is not a deceiver, or that appearances must have causes; and then, by invoking the further principle that there must be some resemblance between cause and effect (and so between reality and appearance) one might guarantee some knowledge of the character, as well as of the existence, of material objects. In general, it is characteristic of the Transcendentalist to admit both unobservable entities and principles which are not empirically testable; by this means he may hope to reinstate, at least in part, the propositions which he was in danger of having to give up.

A very different type of response to the problem was Hume's. Put very baldly, his view was that all our everyday statements about material objects incorporate mistakes in a systematic way, and so none of them can, as they stand, be rationally accepted; hence, of course, claims to know them to be true must be false or absurd. He adds, however, that we are so constituted as human beings that we are incapable of ceasing to make and accept such statements in our everyday life, even though in our reflective moments we may see the error of our ways. We might perhaps confer the label of 'rejector' upon one who, when it is asked how we are to preserve a particular range of everyday assertions from destruction by philosophical argument, replies that such preservation is not rationally possible. The rejector's response is not less metaphysical than the Transcendentalist's.

A more recently fashionable method of dealing with our kind of quandary is the method of reduction. For instance, some philosophers have tried to remove the barrier between sense-impressions and material objects by maintaining that material objects are just collections or families of sense-impressions; or to put the view in a more modern garb, they have suggested that sentences about material objects are translatable, in principle at least, into complicated sentences about the sense-impressions that people actually do have, or would have, in certain conditions. If so much is granted, it would be claimed, there remains no difficulty in the idea that facts about sense impressions constitute a legitimate evidential basis for statements about material objects; for to conclude that since certain sorts of sense-impressions have been obtained in certain sorts of conditions, therefore more or less similar sense-impressions would be obtained in more or less similar conditions, is not more objectionable in principle than to argue (say) from the character of a sample to the character of the population from which the sample is drawn. In general, the procedure of the reducer when faced with a question of the type 'How can we legitimately claim to know about Xs when our only direct information is about Ys' is to reply that the difficulty disappears if we recognize that Xs are nothing over and above Ys, that to talk about Xs is to talk in a concealed way about Ys. Whether we are to count the reductive response as metaphysical or not depends on how seriously it is pressed. If the 'reducer' maintains that his proposed reduction, or something like it, *must* be accepted as the only way of avoiding on the one hand the introduction of transcendental hypotheses, and on the other hand wholesale rejection of a certain class of everyday statements, then he, too, is to be counted as a metaphysician; but if he is prepared to allow his proposed reduction to be treated purely on its merits, and does not regard its acceptance as being the only satisfactory way of meeting some threat to common sense, then he is not a metaphysician. But then, too, he cannot be taking the quandary very seriously: he must be thinking of it as an *apparent* quandary, the illusion of a quandary, which can be dispelled without recourse to any of these drastic measures.

The question arises: How is our characterization of these quandary-responses as metaphysical connected with what we have previously had to say about metaphysics? In more ways than one. In the first place, it is necessary, in order for the quandary to arise at all, and to appear as something requiring drastic measures, that some conceptual shift, some perhaps unnoticed change in our ordinary way of looking at things, should already be occurring. That change of view, on which Wisdom lays such emphasis, is already taking place. Second, behind the quandary and the change of view, we may sometimes glimpse the working of one of those preferences among the categories which we earlier mentioned. For example, it may be that Plato believed in the supreme reality of those eternal changeless entities, the Forms, partly at least because he wished to preserve the possibility of scientific knowledge and yet was threatened with having to reject it; for philosophical reflection made it appear that knowledge of perceptible things was impossible, since perceptible things were constantly in process of change. In order, then, to resolve his quandary, to find a subject-matter for scientific knowledge, Plato was led to introduce, and to exalt, the Forms. But the idea that knowledge of changeable things is impossible, which gives rise to the quandary, may itself arise from a preference: from the feeling that to be unchanging (and so permanent and stable) is so much better than to be changing (and so fleeting and insecure) that only knowledge of unchanging things is *worthy* of the name of knowledge.

We have spoken of some of the springs, and of some of the characteristic features, of metaphysics. Our survey is summary and incomplete. It will be supplemented by more detailed discussion of different aspects of the subject in the essays that follow. But even from a summary survey, a general picture emerges. The enterprise of metaphysics emerges as, above all, an attempt to re-order or to reorganize the set of ideas with which we think about the world; assimilating to one another some things which we customarily distinguish, distinguishing others which we normally assimilate; promoting some ideas to key positions, downgrading or dismissing others. It is supremely a kind of conceptual revision which the metaphysician undertakes, a re-drawing of the map of thought — or parts of it — on a new plan. Of course such revisions are often undertaken *within* particular departments of human thought, and are not then metaphysical ventures. But the revision which the metaphysician undertakes, although it may be undertaken in the interests — or supposed interests — of science, or in the light of history, or for the sake of some moral belief, is always of a different order from a merely departmental revision. For among the concepts he manipulates are always some — like those of knowledge, existence, identity, reality — which, as Aristotle said, are common to all the departmental studies. Partly for this reason, the metaphysical revision tends to comprehensiveness, tends to call for readjustments everywhere. Not that it inevitably issues in a comprehensive system, although it is never merely departmental. For though the notions to be revised are general, and not departmental, notions, they need not all be revised at once and to the limit. So we have those comparatively localized disturbances, where, from the interplay of quandary and preference, there emerges some minor metaphysical shift in the contours of thought. But the metaphysician *par excellence* will not stop short at this. With more or less of boldness, ingenuity and imagination, he re-draws the whole map.

METAPHYSICAL SYSTEMS
(Epistemological)

THAT anything exists at all seems a problem, in itself puzzling. There might have been nothing. Why should there be anything? There must always have been moods when people thought like this and wondered, when they stared at the mere fact of existence, as at a mystery requiring an explanation. If you think of the fact of existence itself as a mystery, then you will soon find yourself looking for an explanation of the universe outside the universe itself; in other words, you will look for a transcendental explanation — for something beyond all existence which explains why anything at all exists. Immanuel Kant gave reasons why it must be a mistake to look for something beyond, which would explain the fact of existence; but not an ordinary mistake, not a simple confusion or a childish weakness, which can be cleared up by straightforward argument. He thought it a necessary propensity of the human mind to look for something beyond all the facts of experience, to press on towards a total explanation whenever, in science, we are offered a partial explanation. We are driven to look, by the nature of human experience, but we cannot find, and the looking and the not finding are not merely psychological weaknesses. Human experience allows only of conditional explanations of

23

things : if so-and-so is given, then so-and-so must follow. This is always the form of scientific explanation. We can never arrive in science at an unconditional explanation of the form, so-and-so must exist, therefore so-and-so must follow. In trying to find such an unconditional explanation of things, we would be trying to apply our categories of explanation outside all possible experience ; for all conceivable experience is experience of a sequence of events in time, the earlier events in the sequence determining the later. We do not even know what would be meant by a kind of experience which did not fall into this form. The word 'experience' itself would have lost all meaning for us. Of course we may string words together in sentences and talk of some necessarily existing being or timeless reality. But if we say anything positive about such timeless realities, we find ourselves talking in a void. Our words are empty. It no longer matters what we assert or what we deny about this timeless reality, which must lie beyond all possible experience. Anything goes ; and there is no way, even in principle, of distinguishing truth from falsity in this kind of discourse ; and this is the same as to say that all statements about transcendental realities are without content, empty. Kant argues that all meaningful uses of language, and all thought, presuppose a certain constant background or context, and they lose all sense and meaning when they are extended outside this context. The forms of language itself show what this context is, and they are what they are because of it. Underneath all the particular grammars of particular languages, there is a deeper grammar which reflects the universal features of human experience, that is, the position of persons as observers in space and time of a succession of events. For instance, we have to think of our experience as an experience of things, existing in space and persisting as the same things through time with changing qualities. This is part of the unavoidable grammar of our thought, equally part of the unavoidable nature of experience. We cannot think it away. But at the same time we are aware of this limitation on our thought and experience as a limitation ; and this is why we are tempted, hopelessly, into metaphysical speculation, trying to break the bonds, as it were, where the bonds are the necessary forms of experience as we know it. All we can do, as philosophers, is to penetrate to this deeper grammar, which reflects the presuppositions of all our thought and experience ; and then we shall realize why it is that our knowledge can never be complete, and why we can never have unconditional explanations of the nature of things, as they are in themselves, apart from the conditions of our experience of them.

Deductive metaphysics, system-building of the old kind, has never recovered from Kant's criticism, and I do not think that it ever will. The old idea that a philosopher might deduce by pure reason what *must* have been the origin of things, and what *must* be the structure of the universe, at least in outline, seems to me to have been killed stone dead. Certainly there have been some flickers of life in deductive metaphysics since ; McTaggart's *Nature of Existence*, for instance, or Samuel Alexander's *Space, Time and Deity*, which is more tentative and less deductive in method than McTaggart's was. But they have not held the interest of philosophers, who have generally been working out the implications of Kant's argument, either pressing it further or in some way qualifying it or amending it. I can think of only one later attempt at a metaphysical system which does take account of Kant's criticism and which therefore does still hold the attention of philosophers: that is Wittgenstein's *Tractatus Logico-Philosophicus*, published in England in 1922. And it is a very odd attempt at a system, since it disavows itself, the author showing that his own system precludes the possibility of any systematic philosophy. He makes it plain that he is attempting the impossible, and the reasons he gives against any systematic metaphysics are almost the same as Kant's. He says, for instance, that we cannot significantly ask questions, or make statements, which involve only formal concepts. We cannot therefore ask about the origin of things or of events, unless we specify things or events of a particular kind. The words 'thing' and 'event' stand for formal concepts, and such concepts are empty or vacuous unless some empirical concept is added to them. This distinction between the material and formal elements of our speech and thought is Kant's distinction; Kant also insisted that concepts are empty if considered apart from all possible application to experience. In his later work, the *Philosophical Investigations*, Wittgenstein went as far as anyone could in repudiating the possibility of any systematic philosophy. The lesson of his later work is that we fall into nonsense, mere idle words, if we consider questions or statements apart from the actual context of human life in which the questions would ordinarily be asked or the statements made. In order to achieve sense in thought and language, it is not enough merely to observe the dictionary definitions of words, the rules of grammar and the laws of logic. The significance of any statement whatever, together with its grammar and its logic, presuppose some constant background of ordinary human interests and purposes and of ordinary human experience. If we try to use ordinary forms of words in some context where this background of ordinary experience is lacking, we find ourselves merely playing with words in a void. For example, if I talk of the feelings and memories of disembodied spirits, I do not necessarily offend against the dictionary definitions of words or against the rules of grammar or of logic. There need be nothing wrong with my words and sentences considered merely as English words and sentences. But when I reflect on what I could mean by hopes and feelings and memories in this extraordinary context, I may find myself unable to say what I could mean; for the ordinary meaning of 'hope' or 'feeling' or 'memory' is so inextricably tied up with the ordinary background of physical existence that I cannot say how I would, or even could, apply these words if persons did not exist as recognizable physical bodies. Perhaps I could give some strange sense to these words in this strange context: I do not know. But at least, it is not obvious what the meaning would be, or what analogy it would bear to the meaning of these words as they are ordinarily used. A systematic metaphysician need not speculate on the immortality of the soul; but he will always, I think, need to use some variant of ordinary language in a context in which the ordinary limitations of human experience are somehow removed. If in his speculations he accepts the limitations of human observers, as persons existing in time, and makes no claim to go beyond them, he would not be called a metaphysician at all; he would simply be a very speculative scientist, or perhaps a speculative historian, and we should wait to see whether any evidence was forthcoming to confirm his speculations. He steps over the limits into the kind of metaphysics which Kant condemned when he starts to tell us about timeless realities and tries to explain the existence of the universe, or the purposes of human life, by reference to them. At this point he should come to a stop and remain silent; that was Wittgenstein's advice. In Kant's phrase, we should realize that we are trying to comprehend the incomprehensible.

But, having followed Kant so far, I must now say that it does not seem to me that he has proved that there is no such thing as metaphysics : only that there is no such thing as transcendental and deductive metaphysics. The difficulty here is not to quarrel about a word, a label. Kant is himself often referred to as a metaphysician. He is prepared to make statements about the necessary presuppositions of all thought and experience ; and this may earn him the title of metaphysician, even though he does not try to deduce from them some system of ultimate reality, as, for example, Spinoza and Leibniz did. A strict empiricist philosopher of the contemporary kind would certainly not say anything about the necessary presuppositions of all thought and experience ; for he would ask how such statements are to be proved or otherwise established as true. If he were very strict indeed, he would not say anything at all of an even remotely metaphysical kind ; he would confine himself to showing metaphysicians that they had not so far attached a sense to their words. But let us forget labels. There is in fact a tradition of philosophical writing which effectively begins with Aristotle and passes through Aquinas and others in the Middle Ages, comes to life again in Descartes, Spinoza and Leibniz, suffers an enormous change in Kant, and continues in this century in the early work of Russell and in Wittgenstein's *Tractatus Logico-Philosophicus*. This is the tradition of systematic philosophy, that is, of philosophy trying to give an account of the necessary structure of human knowledge and of the limits of human knowledge.

In doing this, philosophy finds itself circling round and round certain key notions, which are the organizing notions on which all thought and knowledge depends ; here are some of these organizing notions — Exist, True, Same, Possible and Impossible, Certain and Uncertain, Like and Unlike. It seems, on the evidence of history, that systematic philosophy must come back to these notions and to exploring the relations between them. For they are the most general notions in our language and enter into every kind of discourse. When therefore we enquire into the varying conditions of their application, we get a view of the whole range of our discourse. But if we have the ambitions of a system-builder, we will try to do more than get a view of the range of our thought : we will try to set limits to it, to determine what it should be, or must be, not merely what it actually is. If, for example, we lay down under what conditions we can properly claim to be certain that a statement is true, we are already on the way to constructing a metaphysical system ; for we will have picked out one type of statement of which we can say that the subject-terms stand for something that certainly exists. And then we shall have to explain the existence of everything else in terms of this privileged type of entity, whatever it may be. This is the classical path by which the theory of knowledge has always, since Plato, led directly into system-building. Spinoza and Leibniz both used this argument from the nature of knowledge and of truth in constructing their metaphysical systems ; and so did Russell, when he argued that, outside mathematics, we can only be certain of the truth of statements which describe our own sensations, and therefore that all scientific knowledge must ultimately refer to the order of our sensations. But there is a devastating reply which can be made to system-building of this deductive kind. In the last thirty years philosophers have seen more clearly why the conditions of application of 'certain' and 'uncertain', as of 'same', 'true', 'exist', must vary with every type of term, and with every type of statement, with which they are combined. For the meaning of any expression is determined by the conditions under which we can claim certainty in the application of it. There could not therefore be any *single* set of conditions in which certainty can properly be claimed in respect of *all* expressions, whatever they may be. And for the same reason it must be impossible to find some *general* criterion of identity or of existence or of truth. I think that no philosopher now could follow Descartes, Spinoza and Leibniz in looking for such general criteria. Therefore I do not think that any philosopher now would try to found a metaphysical system on the basis of pure deduction — deduction, that is, from what knowledge must be, or what truth must be, where this is decided by *a priori* reasoning. But the general subject-matter of deductive metaphysics remains, even if the method of handling it must be different, no longer the deductive method. We still want some general view of the scope of human knowledge, of its divisions into different types, and of its outer limits, as far as we can determine them now. And exploring the relations between these most general notions — existence, truth, identity and so on — will provide us with the outlines of the map of human knowledge, and will show what the limits of knowledge are. But, as Kant and Wittgenstein suggested, we have to start on this explanation from the actual human situation which conditions all our thought and language, the situation, that is, of men observing and acting from a particular position in time and space, referring to particular things in their environment, identifying and classifying them, and trying to find ways to alter them. It is characteristic of the great metaphysical systems — Spinoza, Leibniz, for instance — that they culminate in a picture of ideal knowledge which escapes all these limitations ; actual knowledge is seen as an approximation to the complete knowledge which an eternal mind would enjoy, subject to no limitations of viewpoint. F. H. Bradley, writing after Kant and in the critical age of philosophy, admits that ideal and perfect knowledge would not be anything like what we now mean by knowledge; it would be more like feeling, in that the distinction between the knower and the known would have disappeared altogether, and knowledge would no longer be mediated through the forms of language or through our limited categories of thought. It would be direct and intuitive, an identification of the mind with reality. One may think that these are entirely mystical phrases, devoid of literal sense, except possibly as descriptions of some special mystical experiences. But history shows that this is not so; the use of just these phrases is the necessary consequence of following an entirely rational line of argument. For this reason they occur again and again as the culminating point, and as a kind of last chapter, of metaphysical systems: even in the most hard-headed philosophers, such as Spinoza, who certainly was not describing mystical experiences. We have to account for this recurrence, if we are to understand what metaphysical systems are: and not account for them only in William James' way, as the expression of psychological needs, but as the conclusions of severely rational men pushing clear reason to its limits, its limit being just a kind of apparent mysticism and obscurity.

The rational argument, I suggest, goes like this: we distinguish different levels of comprehensiveness and objectivity in our actual knowledge. Knowledge becomes more genuinely knowledge the more comprehensive it is and the less it reflects the viewpoint of the knowing subject. Therefore, at the top of the scale, perfect knowledge would be absolutely comprehensive and it would not reflect the viewpoint of the knowing subject even to the smallest degree; indeed the knowing subject would have no particular viewpoint; he would know things as they are in their own true, objective order. Any actual human knowledge, even of the most comprehensive scientific kind, does still reflect the limitations of the knowing subject. It is not therefore real knowledge of things as they are, in their own true order, but knowledge of things as they appear to us: it is the best we can do, but it is not ideal knowledge. This was Spinoza's argument, and it can be found in various forms in almost all metaphysical systems of the strictly deductive kind.

This argument has only one crucial step: the step of extrapolating to the top of the scale: it is just this step which makes metaphysical systems. Because we know what it is to know something about something, and to know more and more about more and more, it seems that we must be able to say what it would be like to know everything about everything. As we can in fact learn what is the cause of this or that thing, so we can say what it would be like to know the cause of each and everything. It is this unrestricted use of 'all' and 'everything' that is characteristic of the metaphysician. It therefore seems that, if we reject his claims, we must be saying that knowledge is in its very nature limited and must always be incomplete, and that what remains to be known must always be inexhaustible. And this is indeed exactly what I would say. This seems to me to be the real ground for the impossibility of a metaphysical system of a deductive kind : that there can be no sense in the notion of complete knowledge. The objection to deductive metaphysics is not some more or less technical objection of logic ; nor do we need to refer to some special philosophical principle, such as the principle that all statements must be verifiable, in some technical meaning of 'verifiable'. We need only appeal to the conditions in which statements are made and are understood and are known to be true or false. If we suppose these conditions removed, we find that we no longer know what could be meant by 'statement' or 'understanding' or 'knowledge' or 'truth'. If we succeed in stating what these conditions are, we succeed in stating what is meant by 'statement', 'understanding', 'knowledge' and 'truth'. And this would not be a mere discovery about words ; we would have advanced towards that general view of the nature of knowledge at which philosophers are always aiming. But we have to begin from the actual situation of persons, situated at a certain point relative to other things in space and time, using signs to refer and to identify, to ask questions and give orders, and to calculate possible changes in their environment. Given that this is the situation and that these are the needs, various forms of thought and speech may be traced back to these primary needs. But to many contemporary philosophers it seems that Kant was still too dogmatic in picking out just one set of categories or formal elements in our thought. It is rightly said that we can distinguish the formal elements in our thought, and also the human needs which they reflect, in many different ways. Nor can we assume that there is just one universal grammar, consisting of all the elements common to all the grammars of all human languages. But, while admitting this, it still seems to me that Kant was right in looking for some few categories, or elements of grammar, which are the most fundamental of all, and in trying to show some systematic connection between them. Perhaps no one would now claim that there is just one, finally correct way of exhibiting this systematic connection. Rather there is room for a variety of different tentative systems, none of them claiming finality, but each bringing into prominence some very general feature of our discourse. There is no reason why systematic philosophy should also be dogmatic and claim finality for itself; and there is no reason also why it should assume the form of pre-Kantian metaphysics, that is, why it should claim to represent the ultimate nature of reality independent of actual human knowledge.

But perhaps you will say that there is a reason, or, if not a reason, at least a motive, which I have neglected and which certainly inspired the great metaphysical systems of the past: the moral motive. Metaphysical systems have usually led to new moral insights; for to show the nature of reality was to show the place of man in nature, and therefore his proper duties and purposes; it was to show the way to his salvation, to the kind of knowledge that would set him free from his ordinary interests and preoccupations. There seems to be nothing of this kind gained, if as philosophers we try to gain insight into the various forms of human knowledge as it is, accepting their natural limitations. Nothing then follows about how we ought to live. We have been given no view of any ideal kind of life which escapes the ordinary human conditions. We will only have gained a clearer view of the limitations of our actual ways of thought. But does this throw no light on the nature of moral problems and on the questions of how we ought to live ? I think that it does throw light, exactly because problems of life and conduct are, of all problems, the most misrepresented if we neglect the actual limitations of our knowledge and suppose some ideal conditions of living. The great metaphysical systems have sometimes positively misled men by suggesting that there is a level of enlightenment at which all conflicts disappear and choice between good and bad becomes easy, obvious or unnecessary. Any approach to morality, which does not take human limitations as they are, seems to me not only ill-founded, but also evil : evil, because it will lead to disregarding the action which we must take to meet the actual sufferings and passions of people as somehow trivial, on a lower level, and as not philosophically interesting. Spinoza is the great exception — indeed in my opinion the greatest of metaphysical moralists. He tried to show that only by a full scientific and philosophical understanding of the natural order, and of our own passions which are part of the natural order, can we avoid evil and avoid being unhappy and divided. But he also gave reasons why human beings cannot in any case attain to complete knowledge, and so to complete freedom and satisfaction, except in occasional moments. Human beings necessarily have a limited outlook as finite things in nature, and their thought and knowledge are formed by their immediate environment and cannot reflect the whole natural world, except when their thought is directed towards those most essential features of the natural order which are exemplified in every part of it. At these moments, as in mathematical thinking, we are concerned with eternal truth and are free from the influence of our particular environment and from our own particular passions. We can improve our understanding by concentrating our attention on the permanent features of the natural order, and in this way we may come to see our own passions and interests as examples of universal laws. We will understand our previous interests in the particular things around us from a clearer, more objective point of view and will be interested in them in a different, more philosophical way. When we fully understand why we hate and love this or that particular thing, our interest will already have been turned away from the particular thing, as we previously conceived it. The real object of our interest will have changed, since it now presents itself to us in a quite different way. Man can therefore be improved by being taught to think scientifically and philosophically about problems of every kind, including personal problems and problems of politics. The only work of Spinoza published in his lifetime was a treatise on politics, the *Tractatus Theologico-Politicus*, in which he advocates religious toleration and a liberal society; the purpose of political institutions is to provide the possibility of freedom of thought, the framework within which men can develop their powers of reasoning. It was this present life, with all its limitations, and the conditions of actual, living men, that concerned him.

METAPHYSICAL ARGUMENTS

METAPHYSICIANS do not just assert their positions. They attempt to support them by argument, and to give proofs of their conclusions. Some consideration of these proofs must form part of any enquiry into the nature of metaphysics; for it is the attempt to give a proof for his conclusion, to show by logical argument that such-and-such must be so, that chiefly distinguishes the philosophical metaphysician from the mystic, the moralist and others who express or try to express a comprehensive view of how things are or ought to be.

It may well be that the thorough-going metaphysician does not often, psychologically speaking, start with his proofs; he may start rather with a view of the world, and find subsequently demonstrations that articulate his thoughts in the required shape. In this sense, the arguments that he gives may be described as rationalizations — so long as this description does not mean that the arguments are therefore summarily to be dismissed as baseless, invalid or contemptible. Part of the word 'rationalization' is after all the word 'rational', and it is in virtue of their logical structure, their claims to logical validity, that metaphysical theories are marked off from mere intuitive and unformulated insights into reality.

39

However, the resemblance of metaphysical theories to rationalizations in the psychoanalytical sense does go rather deeper than this, and it may make one wonder whether the arguments that the metaphysician produces really *matter*. To some recent writers, metaphysical theories and arguments have seemed to be just symptoms of a kind of intellectual neurosis or 'mental cramp' [1] — the metaphysician is a man with an *idée fixe* which he projects on the world in the form of an ambitious and distorted theory. So, just as it is no good reasoning with a neurotic, it is no good arguing with a metaphysician — what one must do, in both cases, is to cure them. Hence there goes with this view of metaphysics a corresponding view of the proper duty of philosophy. The philosopher should play psychoanalyst to the tortured and theory-ridden metaphysician and, by-passing the arguments in which he rationalizes his worries, use analytic technique to get to the roots of the worries themselves.

In its extremer forms, this view seems to be a wild exaggeration. What it rightly emphasizes is that many important metaphysical arguments are not the sort of arguments that can just be accepted as valid or rejected as invalid by certain and generally agreed rules, and that their value or their faults are likely to lie deeper, in some central concept or idea which the metaphysician is trying to articulate through them. The weakness of this therapeutic

---

[1] This phrase, and the underlying idea, come from Wittgenstein. The most thorough-going exponent of the theory is John Wisdom — see his collection of articles, *Philosophy and Psychoanalysis*, published by Blackwell.

view, if taken a long way, is that there seems to be
no reason why it should not be taken all the way,
so that metaphysics comes to be regarded, not just
as *like* a neurosis, but as being indeed a particular
sort of neurosis. If it were so regarded, of course,
the use of philosophy or philosophical analysis to
cure it would be a frivolous pursuit — what would
be needed would be real psychoanalysis. One cannot seriously believe that metaphysics is as non-
rational as this, or that philosophers should really
hand over to the clinicians. The analysis that is
required is philosophical, not psychological, and
what requires it is not the metaphysician himself but
his arguments; which should be taken seriously as
rational attempts to prove a point of view.

Of course, metaphysicians vary in the extent to
which they try to give proofs of what they say; and
in the extent to which the proofs that are given are
precisely and rigorously expressed; and in the extent
to which the proofs, however expressed, form an
essential part of the thought, and are not just there
for decoration. To take two comparable British
metaphysicians, for instance, there is a marked
difference between McTaggart and Bradley: while
McTaggart seeks knock-down forms of proof and
hard coal-like knobs of argument, Bradley tentatively
adumbrates. Yet allowing for all these differences,
there is in practically any Western metaphysician of
importance a core of argument, an attempt to support
his position or raise his questions by a movement
from premises to conclusion.

All theorists employ arguments and make inferences, for all are concerned to get from one place to

another, to move from a set of premises or collection of facts to a conclusion. But, equally notoriously, not all theorists make the same kind of inferences, and a movement from premises to conclusion can be made according to very different sorts of rules. Logicians, who have been concerned to examine, classify and formalize the different types of inference, have divided them by a basic distinction into two broadly different classes — inductive and deductive inferences. Deductive inferences are such that if you accept the premises, you must accept the conclusion, or else contradict yourself — the conclusion follows with rigorous logical necessity from what implies it. Such are the arguments, for instance, of mathematicians. Inductive arguments, on the other hand, have no such absolute rigour ; one who accepted the premises would not *contradict* himself if he refused to accept the conclusion, although he might look pretty silly. Most practical inferences of everyday life are of this type : thus if a man arrives from personal experience at the conclusion that it is always unwise to play cards with strangers on race trains, he is making an inductive step.

This example points to one further important feature of inductive arguments. The man who arrives at this conclusion is *generalizing* — he is saying something to the effect : 'Seven times I've been asked to play, and seven times they've tried to swindle me — so probably next time, or any other time, I'm asked, it will be the same'. His argument so far is very sound, but of course he may be wrong in his conclusion ; it is always *possible* that the next card-playing stranger may be honest. This is a general feature of inductive arguments. Just because it is their function to lead from some matter of fact already accepted to some wider, or at least different, assertion, their conclusions are always in a sense only probable. An inductive inference is empirical, and it is always conceivable that its conclusion should turn out to be untrue, however carefully it has been considered.

In the case of deductive arguments the situation is more complicated. Deductive arguments can have conclusions that are necessary and certain — such are the conclusions of mathematical arguments. But they will be so only if the premisses are certain as well, just because a deductive argument gives you no more in the conclusion than what is already tied up or implied in the premisses. If the premisses are only probable, then so will the conclusion be. The immediate point for the present discussion, however, is that inductive arguments can lead only to empirical and probable results.

What is the relation of metaphysical arguments to these two sorts of argument? An enquiry into this relation should at least help us to see what a metaphysical argument is not, and may help us to see something of what it is. It is clear, first, that metaphysicians do not characteristically make straightforward inductive inferences: they do not say things of the form 'such and such is true in these instances, so it is probably always true'. It would be absurd, for instance, to suppose that a metaphysician would reach the conclusion 'men have freewill' by an argument like 'all men we have observed have freewill, so men in general do' as one might argue 'all the men we have observed have eyebrows, so men in general do'. The *a priori* quality of a metaphysical conclusion, its necessity, by itself makes such a procedure inappropriate: there could be no need of *that* kind of support from experience.

Yet it must be said that some arguments that metaphysicians have employed do look remarkably like inductive inferences. Such, for example, is the simplest form of the theological argument from design, once well known under the name of 'Paley's watch'. Paley's form of it was just this: 'If we found by chance a watch or other piece of intricate mechanism we should infer that it had been made by someone. But all around us we do find intricate pieces of natural mechanism, and the processes of the universe are seen to move together in complex relations; we should therefore infer that these too have a Maker.' There are some general difficulties about an argument from analogy of this type; but the immediate point is that it does seem just to be a kind of inductive argument. Paley's reasoning is simply this: 'wherever in the past we have found intricate mechanisms we have found a maker, so in this case, too, we can infer one'. But by being an inductive argument it seems too weak for its purpose. For, taken by itself, it can lead only to an inductive type of conclusion; and so the statement of the existence of a God, to which it is supposed to lead, will have the status only of a quasi-scientific hypothesis; and for any such inductive hypothesis, as we have seen, the opposite involves no contradiction, and is logically possible. So one who from *this* type of argument accepted the existence of God would have to admit that it was at least possible that God did not exist after all. But in general one who believed in God would not admit that it was in any way possible that God did not exist; he would insist that the statement of God's existence must have some sort of absolute necessity. Thus Paley's watch, if it is to be called a metaphysical argument at all, does not seem to be a characteristic one, nor yet a characteristic argument for the existence of God. It is only, as it were, a super-scientific inference.

Another way of saying that the metaphysician does not use inductive arguments is to point out that in metaphysical conclusions the notion of probability plays no part. As we have seen, it is a characteristic of inductive inferences that the word 'probably' can always slip into them. But the metaphysician does not offer his conclusions as being *probably* so; he argues that they *must* be so. Here again, we do meet what look like exceptions to this rule. In the earlier writings of Bertrand Russell, for instance, we find him saying things like this: 'there are arguments that try to show that the external world does not exist, but since these arguments are not conclusive, and we have a natural tendency to believe that the external world does exist, we are probably safer in going on thinking that it does'. Professor Broad and others have written in a similar vein, as if weighing the probability of one metaphysical thesis against another.

I should like to make two points about this type of example. First, I think there certainly is, or has been, a way of doing philosophy that tried to

45

assimilate it to the natural sciences, and hence regarded its conclusions in the light of probabilities. Some philosophers in this century, impressed by the achievements of the sciences and depressed by traditional metaphysics, sought to apply scientific methods inside philosophy itself, and the results did include what look like metaphysical conclusions presented with an air of inductive probability. I think, however, that if these arguments are closely examined, they can be found not to be straightforward inductive arguments, as Paley's perhaps was; the language of theory and probability is little more than a dressing for a philosophical conceptual argument. Moreover, these philosophers are not typical metaphysicians; they themselves, I suspect, might have denied that what they were doing was metaphysics.

Second, there may be another reason, quite different from the last, why Russell, for instance, should qualify metaphysical conclusions with terms like 'probably'. We have already seen one reason why the conclusion of an argument should be thought to be only probable: that is, just that the argument is an inductive one, and a philosopher may want to mark the empirical nature of any inductive argument by inserting 'probably' into it. If this is what Russell meant, then certainly his argument is an inductive one. But this is only one reason why the word 'probably' should occur in an argument, and there are others. Another, and very familiar, reason is that the premisses of the argument are themselves only probable, in the quite ordinary sense in which, for instance, it is (at best) only probable that the favourite will win the 2.30 at tomorrow's races. Of course, if my premisses are only probable, then any conclusion I draw from them, even in deductive argument, will be only probable. As we noticed before, you get no more out of deduction than you put in at the beginning. Thus, if someone thinks that the favourite will probably win the 2.30, he can infer, validly if uninterestingly, that probably no other horse will; but he will get no conclusion that is itself certain, since his premisses already are no more than probable. Here we have a reason why the word 'probably' should occur even in deductive arguments. But again, if we look back at Russell's argument, it is not of *this* pattern; his premisses — *e.g.* that we believe in an external world — are not in themselves dubious, as forecasts about tomorrow's races are.

Still, there is yet another way in which 'probably' can come into an argument, and this may shed more light on Russell's. In considering an argument, we may be concerned not so much with the question of whether the premisses and the conclusion are true or false, certain or probable, as with the question of whether the conclusion follows from the premisses — that is, we may just want to know whether the argument is *valid*. Strictly speaking, there are no degrees of validity: the conclusion either follows from the premisses or it does not, and there is no middle way. It makes no sense to say that a conclusion 'more or less' or 'just about' follows. Yet one often meets the situation in which one is not *sure* whether a given argument is valid. The premisses may be complicated or unclearly expressed, the chain of reasoning subtle, and so on, and one may be in genuine doubt whether the conclusion does follow or not. In such cases, one may express one's doubts by saying that the conclusion 'perhaps' or 'probably' follows from the premises.

This sort of doubt, and hence this sort of 'probably', can come in, of course, with any sort of argument, inductive or deductive : a piece of mathematics, for instance, may be so complicated and so little self-evident that the best one can say, pending a lot of further investigation, is that the conclusion is probably reached by valid argument. Russell's argument, and some other metaphysical arguments that involve the notion of probability, may be of this last type. The notion of probability comes into them not because the philosopher thinks that either his conclusion or his premises are inherently dubious, but because he is doubtful about the connection between them — he is not sure whether his conclusion in fact follows. Such doubts, as we have seen, can arise with any sort of argument ; and the fact that a philosopher does not commit himself to saying more than that his conclusion *perhaps* follows, does not by itself show what sort of conclusion he is reaching, or by what sort of argument.

Anyway, metaphysical arguments do not seem to be characteristically inductive. Are they then deductive ?

Deduction seems a better candidate for the metaphysician's professional tool, for deductive arguments can at least lead to conclusions of necessity, which are what he wants. It is commonly said that metaphysicians seek to deduce the nature of reality or some such thing ; and so the impression may be given that the metaphysician's is a wholly deductive enterprise. This impression seems to get support from the great systems that some metaphysicians have constructed, which claim to show deductive relations between features of reality.

But the idea that the metaphysical activity consists just of making deductions in a system neglects a more fundamental question. Every deductive movement must be made from one place to another: one needs both premises and conclusion. So in a chain or system of deductions there must be something at the beginning from which the whole series of reasonings starts. In a formal logical system what one has at the beginning are axioms; these are, relative to that system, unquestionable. They are not themselves derived in the system — there is nothing to derive them from. It is possible to have a number of purely formal systems, each with its own axioms, and for particular purposes one can take one's choice. But the metaphysician is not concerned to give us a choice. He wants to make a series of statements that will both have content and be necessarily true. But if his conclusions are, as he wishes, to be inescapable, and he is deducing the conclusions ultimately from axioms, then the axioms must be inescapable as well — inferences, unlike divers, do not gain in weight as they get nearer the bottom. But the axioms cannot themselves be proved in the system; so the metaphysician must have some other method of supporting his axioms, outside the system. He will try to show that one has to accept his axioms, for only so can he show that one has to accept his conclusions. The weapon he uses to try to make one accept the axioms is in the strongest sense the metaphysical argument.

The rationalist system-builders of the seventeenth century tried in their different ways to find axioms for their systems which would be inescapable; but their method was on the whole to look for axioms which needed no support of any kind, which were self-evidently true. So their metaphysical argument at this point is rather an appeal to propositions which need no argument at all. Thus Descartes, for instance, by his procedure of systematic doubt, whittled away the truths he believed in until he arrived at the apparently indubitable truth 'I am doubting', from which he took an immediate step to 'I exist'. Whether he regarded this step as purely deductive is to me unclear; at any rate, the indubitability of 'I am doubting' seemed to him to be established by the pure light of reason.

But not all system-builders use methods as simple as this to provide their axioms. And not all metaphysicians are, in this most ambitious sense, system-builders. Our argument has shown why there is no need for them to be. For if a metaphysical argument can be used to compel one to accept a statement which is then going to be used as the axiom of a system, it can also be used to make one accept the statement even if it is not going to be used as an axiom. Even metaphysicians not engaged in comprehensive system-building will try to show by constructive argument that such and such (which on the whole you didn't expect) must be so; or, very frequently, by destructive argument, that so

and so (which on the whole you did expect) can't
be so. I shall in a moment try to say something
about the interrelation of these in a typical case.

In contrasting, up to this point, arguments used
by metaphysicians with inductive and with deductive
arguments, I have spoken as if there were one
definite sort of argument that is metaphysical. I
think in fact there is no one thing that is a metaphysical argument, just as there is no one thing that
is a metaphysical statement. This does not mean,
however, that absolutely no general remarks can be
made about them; only that such general remarks
will serve to characterize these arguments in outline
rather than to state some one essential property of
them. One essential property of them, however,
can be and has been stated : that they are not the
same as deductive or inductive arguments. For some
philosophers, indeed, such as the so-called logical
positivists, this is quite enough; all metaphysical
arguments and statements are by them lumped
together and dismissed as meaningless. But this
skeletal unity tells us nothing about metaphysics;
it is only the uniformity of all before the final leveller.
The approach of these collectively anti-metaphysical
philosophers is a kind of philosophical parallel to
the attitude of a fanatically militarist person who
divides all men into two classes only, combatants
and non-combatants. Even from the military point
of view, such a division would have its disadvantages :
among non-combatants, for instance, it fails to distinguish between the medically unfit and the conscientious objectors. A metaphysician, in relation
to the positivist criterion of meaning, is more like a

conscientious objector than like an invalid; it is
his whole purpose to do something other than what
the positivist wants him to do. And just as there
are different kinds of conscientious objector, so there
are different types of metaphysician and of metaphysical argument. Understanding can only be
gained by taking individual cases.

Within the limits of this chapter it is possible to
look at only one example of metaphysical argument
in more detail. It has the overwhelming dis-
advantage of being only one example; but it is
such a central and recurrent one that I hope it may
yield some general lessons as well.

The stage is set for the argument I am going to
consider by the facts of perceptual illusion. All
around us we see objects which we recognize as
being of certain sorts — trees, tables, people and so
on. Occasionally, in the business of recognizing
things, we are deceived, and take something that
we see for something which in fact it isn't. Thus
an old boot in the dusk might be taken for a small
cat. Into this setting the philosopher steps. He
may be concerned with any of a number of questions,
such as 'What do we really know?'; 'How much
reliance can be placed on perception as a source of
knowledge?'; 'What really exists?'; and so on.
But whatever his particular question, his reasoning
from the situation of perceptual illusion may well go
something like this. 'You were deceived when you
took that boot for a cat. Since you were deceived,
there can have been no *intrinsic* difference between
the experience you had at the moment of seeing
what was in fact a boot in the dusk and the experience

you could have had in really seeing a cat at that moment. The difference, after all, came out later — when you had a closer look, made a noise, or whatever it was. Clearly there can be no intrinsic difference between the two experiences, for if there were, you could have told the difference, and would not have taken the one thing for the other. So what was this experience you had? Clearly not that of seeing a cat, for there was no cat to be seen. But equally clearly the experience you had wasn't just that of seeing an old boot, either. For we have already agreed that it must have been the same experience as you could have had in really seeing a cat, for otherwise you couldn't have mistaken the boot for a cat; and if you could have had this experience in really seeing a cat, the experience can't just be that of really seeing a boot; for when you really see a cat you don't really see a boot. So the experience you have in both cases must be something neutral between really seeing a cat and really seeing a boot — it is something common to both and less than either. Moreover' (this philosopher might continue) 'the having of visual experience must be more basic than the seeing of real objects; for one can have visual experiences without in fact seeing the appropriate, or indeed any, sort of object, but we cannot see an object without having visual experiences.'

So runs the argument from illusion in one of its many forms. It contains both a destructive and a constructive movement; both are typical of metaphysical argument. The destructive movement consists of showing that something we should naturally say if asked to reflect on perception — that is, that we just see objects — is false. It may be said that there is nothing very surprising about this, and that anyone who said that we always, whenever we see anything, see a material object, would obviously be wrong; but that nevertheless we sometimes see material objects. But the destructive movement is stronger than this. The metaphysician does not in fact claim that there is *no* difference between being deceived and not being deceived; his argument is just that the difference is not where you expected it to be. For the argument purports to show that by reflection on the cases of illusion we can come to see that the cases of genuine perception as well are different from what we thought; that in these, too, the visual experience of the observer — which, the metaphysician will go on to argue, is private to the observer — must play a part.

To say this, however, is already to have started the constructive movement of the argument. It is characteristic of metaphysical arguments that the method of destruction already points to what is to take the place of the things destroyed. Hence it is that what is in one sense the same argument — an argument, at any rate, generated by the same facts of experience — can appear in different forms in different philosophers to suit their several purposes. The form in which I have presented the argument from illusion (and some particular form had to be chosen) is in fact one that can lay the foundations for an empiricist metaphysic using the notion of an 'idea' or a 'sensation'.

But the same argument can be used for ends quite different from those of the empiricist metaphysician. Plato, for instance, accepted something like the first stage of the argument, and reasoned from this that our beliefs about the material world must be personal, fleeting and unstable. He added the premisses that true knowledge must be of the unchanging and stable, and that we can up to a point have knowledge, and reached the conclusion that there must be a world of unchanging things, the world of Forms. What he and the empiricists have in common is the use of the argument to destroy a world taken for granted and to substitute something else for it — in his case, a world of Forms, in theirs a succession of experiences from which objects have in some way to be inferred or constructed. Here we see a prime characteristic of metaphysical argument — its use to establish propositions of existence or non-existence. 'The world of Forms is the world of genuine existence'; 'the ultimate constituents of the world are sense-data': these are (very different) metaphysical statements a main prop of which is the argument we have been examining.

How is this argument related to the distinction between inductive and deductive arguments? Clearly it is not just inductive: the empiricist metaphysician, for instance, is not just saying 'there are illusions, so probably objects don't exist and individual experiences do'. Yet he is making a movement beyond what he started with. By examining the concept of perceptual illusion, he arrives at a general conclusion about perception as such; a conclusion which is to be attacked, not by the production of any straightforward empirical counter-examples, but by an enquiry into his concepts, in particular the rather dubious concept of 'an experience'.

'Well', someone might say, 'all we have in this argument is a contingent fact and a set of deductions. The deductions are made from the concept of a perceptual illusion; the contingent fact is that the concept has application — that is, we are sometimes deceived.' But this would be a complete misunderstanding. For neither is the supposed contingent fact just a contingent fact, nor are the supposed deductions just deductions. When the metaphysician says, with a disingenuous air of factual simplicity, 'We are sometimes deceived, and take one thing for another', he is not just stating a contingent fact, something that might well be otherwise. All he actually needs for his argument is the logical possibility of misrecognition, the existence of such a concept; and, very roughly, contained in the concept of recognition is the possibility of misrecognition. So long as we have the concept of recognizing things, we must also have that of failing to recognize them. Of course, we might *perhaps* have neither concept; but what our perception would then seem to be is totally obscure. In the relation of recognition and similar concepts to our experience lies a huge philosophical problem. Again, the deductions are not just deductions. If they were, there could scarcely be the disagreement there is with the conclusion; and, again, the metaphysician has acquired from somewhere *en route* a concept with which he did not start out, that of 'an experience'.

Yet the introduction of this concept is not just

gratuitous. It seems to be somehow implied in what is already said, to be demanded by the facts as they stand, and one principal aim of the metaphysician's argument is to display the facts so as to show where the demand comes. The purpose of the argument is not just to deduce a conclusion from the facts. It is rather to show that the account of those facts, when we reflect on them, has a hole in it, a hole which is exactly fitted by the metaphysician's special concept. This concept may be one, like that of 'an experience', which exists already in a rough form in our ordinary language, and which the metaphysician takes up, dignifies and refines into a principle of explanation. Alternatively, if he is a very thorough-going metaphysician, the concepts he uses in this way may be much more technical and remote from ordinary thinking, like Leibniz's 'monads' or Kant's 'noumenal objects'.

The greatness of a metaphysician, it seems to me, is to be determined by three considerations: how arbitrary his special concepts are, how much they explain, and how much they distort our ordinary thinking. These considerations are not, of course, independent — they are bound up together rather like the design requirements of an aeroplane, where conflicting demands such as minimum weight, maximum capacity and the requirements of safety have to be reconciled by expert designers. The designer of genius gets as near as possible to having the best of all worlds, and so does the metaphysical genius. His concepts will explain a lot, by revealing important analogies between kinds of experience and thought which superficially seem widely different.

These analogies must be real ones, and not the product of forced or over-distorting assimilations; and they must not be arbitrary, in the further sense that one must be led to recognize them, and with them the demand for the metaphysician's explanatory concepts, by clear and cogent argument.

But it is the argument that concerns us here, rather than the features of the metaphysician's enterprise when it is completed. Any account of such arguments in a few words is bound to be a caricature, but their standard features can be summarized like this. The metaphysician feels an inconsistency or difficulty or incompleteness in what we naturally tend to think about some feature of our experience, or rather in what seems to be presupposed by what we so think. In resolving this, he will try to show that some concept on which we rely is secondary to, or presupposed by, some other concept which he has introduced or extended from elsewhere. This concept of his may have a special place in the answer to the problem in question (like the empiricists' use of 'experience'), or he may use it widely elsewhere (like Plato's Forms) to solve other problems; the more widely he uses it elsewhere, the more systematic will his philosophy be.

The compulsiveness of his argument will come from his starting with concepts and features of experience which, it seems, must be there if we are to think about our experience at all. His attempt to show that some concept involves a difficulty, or is presupposed by some other concept, will often issue in statements of existence or non-existence. Yet his assertions of existence or non-existence, unlike assertions of either empirical or mathematical existence, are in a sense only comparative. For all metaphysicians agree that appearance, those features of the world which are metaphysically shown to be unreal, must eventually find *some* place in the account of things as they really are. We saw this before in the empiricist's preservation, in a different place, of the ordinary distinction between illusion and genuine perception. Even McTaggart's famous demonstration of the unreality of time (which is both philosophically spectacular and very hard to refute) is preparatory to an account of what it is that really does exist and presents itself to us confusedly as the passage of time. Hence it is that some have seen the metaphysician's activity as primarily one of reallocation: the extension of some favoured concept to a primary place in the account of things at the expense of more familiar concepts.

There is truth in this; yet the choice of such a concept, and the point of its application, is not just arbitrary — and we are left with the problem of why some work so much better than others. Metaphysical arguments are like trees. Their exact position, and their shape, are to a certain extent matters of preference: the metaphysician can choose where exactly to plant them, and how to trim them. But he cannot choose whether they will grow or not; some spots on the conceptual landscape are more fertile than others. If with the positivist axe we chop the trees down, they grow again. If with the Wittgensteinian spade we start digging up the roots, we shall, fascinatedly, go on and on. For even if we dig up one set of roots, there will be, if it was a stout tree, many others. Perhaps digging is the proper philosophical activity at this time — certainly mere pride in having grown a tree larger than anyone else's is no longer enough. But there was something that justified such pride — the knowledge that the metaphysician's green fingers had found the spot where acorns could grow. What spurs on the philosophical digger is the desire to know more. What makes metaphysical trees grow? Why from some features of our experience rather than others do metaphysical arguments spring up? The answer to that question would be the ultimate metaphysical answer.

SCIENCE AND METAPHYSICS

THE title of the present essay may suggest that instances of thinking in metaphysical terms are as easily located as are samples of scientific thought. However, it will perhaps have become clear that philosophers disagree on the exact location of metaphysical thinking proper. Take, for instance, the idea expressed by the phrase, 'same cause, same effect'. Often it is said that the principle underlying this idea forms the very basis of scientific reasoning by justifying us to draw valid conclusions from limited evidence. Thus, in a recent work on the methods of physical science, H. Margenau writes:

Causality is indeed one of the metaphysical requirements of physical theory. . . .[1]

Yet, might we not have said with equal justice that this principle was simply a very general belief held almost instinctively by everyone; or alternatively, that it was a postulate laid down for certain pragmatic purposes? Indeed, Margenau later in the same work shifts in this direction when he writes:

The force of the principle of causality is methodological . . . [it is] continually reinjected into constructive scientific procedures.[2]

[1] H. Margenau, *The Nature of Physical Reality: A Philosophy of Modern Physics*, 1954, p. 94.   [2] *Ibid.* p. 407.

It will be seen that a decision respecting the location of metaphysics is itself something that may become a matter for philosophical argument.

Let us consider a related case. Bertrand Russell, in his *Analysis of Matter*, says that the principle on which logical scientific procedure depends is 'that the simplest law which fits the known facts will also fit the fact to be discovered hereafter'.[1] Of this principle he says that it is simply a postulate which defines the scope of science. There isn't anything metaphysical about this. However, the argument might have been put in a different form. We might have said, since science depends on the possibility of discovering simple laws, and since it clearly exists, therefore nature must be simple. So an 'insight' into the nature of science may be expressed as an insight into nature. It was in this spirit that Galileo wrote:

Nature acts through immutable laws which she never transgresses.

And again:

Nature . . . does not that by many things which may be done by few.[2]

Now we feel that Galileo's statements though perhaps having a cash-value similar to Russell's have a different flavour. They seem to involve something that might be expressed as the conversion of a methodological rule into a factual statement. Consider another remark of Galileo's when he says that

[1] B. Russell, *The Analysis of Matter*, 1954, pp. 233, 237.
[2] Quoted in E. A. Burtt, *The Metaphysical Foundations of Modern Science*, 1932, p. 64.

the 'Universe . . . is written in the mathematical language'.[1] It has been argued that this expresses part of Galileo's metaphysical presuppositions of science. Yet, again one might look at it merely as a peculiar way of postulating that a proper study of physics and astronomy should be carried out with the aid of mathematics. Of course, it is arguable whether one version does reduce to the other. One might say that Galileo did not only want to suggest that the world was somehow particularly suited to mathematical study but believed that mathematics was grounded in the very structure of nature. The question of the equivalence of these two formulations is clearly once more a matter for philosophical argument. To characterize Galileo's assertion as metaphysical is to take a stand at a certain point in this argument. This should be remembered in what follows where I shall be concerned to show what I hold to be characteristically 'metaphysical' about an assertion such as Galileo's. I use the word 'assertion' advisedly because it mirrors admirably something basically involved in the nature of metaphysical statements. For they appear to straddle two conflicting tendencies in our thinking: avowal, recommendation, postulation, on the one hand; description, information, on the other.

II

I want to show then how metaphysical assertions arise out of reflections on the nature of scientific reasoning. A science in its developed stages involves

[1] *Ibid.*

more than mere aided or unaided observation. It also includes a considerable superstructure of connecting elements such as theories, laws and theoretical concepts. Without free conceptual construction facts by themselves could never yield any scientific knowledge.

But reflection on the processes of theorizing in the sciences persistently and almost inevitably has produced certain kinds of quandaries. The resulting puzzles express themselves in three different contexts. They involve the nature of the explanatory concepts or elements which almost any developed theory has to employ, for instance atoms and forces, libido and genes. Secondly, they involve the logical status of the laws which form the basis of every such theory. And finally, the puzzles bear on the nature of theories as such, considered as explanations. In what follows, I shall choose illustrations from each of these contexts in turn.

Consider the particular entities with which a physical theory operates such as atoms, protons, electrons; or connectives such as forces, energies, entropy. Now we want to say two things about these which appear to be in conflict. As an example let us study the case of the atom. We want to say that from the point of view of science, atoms function as fundamental building blocks of the universe. On the other hand, when we reflect we also want to say that we possess only more or less indirect evidence for their existence, and that our knowledge of them connects only in a very complicated way with what alone is directly given to us; namely, various experimental situations. This tempts us into a view the reverse of the first.

How does this conflict connect with metaphysics? At the beginning of the nineteenth century John Dalton put forward an atomic theory in order to account for certain laws of combination between chemical elements — for instance the law, 'chemical elements combine only in fixed and constant proportions by weight'. So we might say that the weight of a certain standard element was equivalent to so many multiples of that of the others. Now Sir Humphry Davy, a celebrated chemist and contemporary of Dalton, objected to the postulation of atoms because, so he held, we have evidence only for the equivalence of the weights of elements but none for the atoms which were assumed to make them up and account for the constancy of the weight ratios.

Here it is important to note a distinction. My simple example shows that up to this point the evidence for atoms was both incomplete as well as indirect. When subsequently it becomes increasingly complete, it remains and to some extent must remain indirect. This is one of the important facts which lead to the conflict of views to be described.

As time went on, particularly during the 1860's and 1870's, the atomic theory received strong support both from the development of the kinetic theory of gases in the hands of Maxwell, Boltzmann and others, as well as the successful modification and employment of Dalton's own theory in the hands of the chemists; not to mention researches beginning in the 1890's culminating in a successful adaptation of atomic concepts (electron) to the phenomenon of electric discharge in gases (J. J. Thomson, 1897–9).

Now, if the existence of the atom is an empirical question one would certainly want to say that these developments strengthened the atomic hypothesis. What then were the reactions of contemporary scientists and philosophers of science? Not all of them were favourable, and it is the unfavourable ones that must interest us here. I shall compare just two important thinkers who were the spokesmen for many who towards the end of the century were still rejecting the idea that there were such things as atoms in nature. One was Wilhelm Ostwald, the important analytical chemist, who as late as 1902 wrote of the atomic or molecular elements of kinetic theory as an 'unproven assumption' and rejected 'the hypothetical representation of heat as a mode of motion' of material particles [1] for a number of reasons too complex to be discussed here. The other man was Ernst Mach, the famous physicist, psychologist and philosopher of science who in his *Science of Mechanics* (1883) had written:

Atoms cannot be perceived by the senses; like all substances they are things of the thought . . . [and] a mathematical *model* for facilitating the mental reproduction of the facts.[2]

Between the years 1903–12 considerable further advances took place. Of special importance for our question was Einstein's work of 1905 in which calculations that involve the assumption of molecular impacts resulting in the so-called 'Brownian motion' of small visible particles suspended in a liquid, led to predictions which were subsequently verified

[1] W. Ostwald, *Vorlesungen über Naturphilosophie*, 1902, p. 204.
[2] E. Mach, *Science of Mechanics*, 1942, p. 590.

experimentally by the work of Perrin and others (1906–8). At the same time, first Wilson (1903) and then Millikan (1910) obtained exceedingly accurate values of the exact amount of electric charge carried by the electron. All this evidence proved clinching for Ostwald. In a new preface to the 1909 edition of his *Allgemeine Chemie* he admitted that he was 'now convinced' that we had 'become possessed of experimental evidence' of the atomic nature of matter, and that even 'the most cautious scientist' was justified 'in now speaking of the experimental proof of the atomic theory of matter'.[1]

Quite different was Mach's reaction. As late as 1915, a year before his death, there is a note from his hand in which he says that he '[cannot] accept the existence of atoms and other such dogma'.[2] I think we may conclude that in this case no developments in science would have been capable of changing his views. These, though originally concerned with an empirical problem, came to turn on a different sort of consideration; one which connected with a different conception of existence (or, if you like, with different ideas respecting the 'concept of existence'). This is suggested by the passage from the *Mechanics* which harps on the indirectness of the evidence and on the fact that atoms 'cannot be perceived by the senses'. Behind Mach's view lies the doctrine that nothing can count as real or existent except an element of sensation.

Unfortunately, this assertion itself — no matter what its origin — must sooner or later become non-

---

[1] W. Ostwald, *Grundriss der allgemeinen Chemie*, 1909, Preface.
[2] E. Mach, *op. cit.* p. xxvi.

empirical. For, what is to count as an element of sensation? Let us consider another hint. Mach, when discussing the refraction of light, writes:

In nature there is no *law* of refraction, only different cases of refraction.[1]

However, an individual case of refraction would still be something rather abstract, complex and general. It is not at all clear whether this could function satisfactorily as a candidate for an 'element of sensation', *i.e.* for something that was fundamental and immediate, against something derivative and constructed. If we cannot tell clearly in the present instance, can we ever tell? What would be the right sort of criteria? Is there not something intrinsically arbitrary about these assertions? At any rate, one thing will have emerged: this is no longer a matter on which scientific considerations have any bearing. In order to stress this point consider some other writers who illustrate it further. Already in the 1840's William Whewell, the Cambridge mineralogist and historian of science, had argued against the atomic hypothesis by claiming the question to be purely a philosophical matter.

When we would assert this theory, not as a convenient hypothesis for the expression or calculation of the laws of nature, but as a philosophical (elsewhere: physical) truth respecting the constitution of the universe, we find ourselves checked by difficulties of reasoning which we cannot overcome, as well as by conflicting phenomena which we cannot reconcile.[2]

[1] E. Mach, *op. cit.* p. 583.
[2] W. Whewell, *The Philosophy of the Inductive Sciences*, 1840, vol. i, p. 414.

As another example, Bridgman, the American Philosopher of science and physicist, could still write in 1927 that the atom was only 'a construct, and its existence entirely inferential', despite the fact that in the same breath he affirmed that we 'are as convinced of its physical reality as of our hands and feet'.[1]

Still more clearly, this irrelevance of the bearing of empirical evidence on our question comes out in a passage occurring in a recent work. *Robert Grosseteste and the Origins of Experimental Science*, by A. C. Crombie.

A scientific theory [he says] . . . tells us no more than it appears to tell us about the experimental facts, namely that they may be related in a particular manner. It can provide no grounds for the belief that the entities postulated for the purposes of the theory actually exist. . . . So . . . a scientific theory has no metaphysical implications.[2]

We see here that in order to decide what exists ultimately and 'in nature' we must (as metaphysicians) pass beyond empirical criteria. But, so we want to ask, can we so pass; and why should we? Let me first consider two possible criticisms which urge that we can not. A reviewer of the book last mentioned (S. Toulmin) replied by asserting that

Scientists certainly claim the right to distinguish, on empirical not metaphysical grounds between those theoretical entities which actually exist and those which are only fictions.[3]

[1] P. W. Bridgman, *The Logic of Modern Physics*, 1927, p. 59.
[2] A. C. Crombie, *Robert Grosseteste and the Origins of Experimental Science*, 1953, p. 319.
[3] S. Toulmin, in *Mind*, vol. 63, 1954, p. 556.

Now Crombie had of course been aware of the scientists' claim to make the distinction between fact and fiction. What he meant was that whatever the distinctions made *within* science, these could not be decisive for the question of the existence of bona-fide scientific entities as such. In other words, he had passed beyond science.

Still, perhaps something more far reaching is implied by this criticism. For one might suggest that though people attempt to pass beyond science in the way described, such a feat is surely *impossible*. And one might want to urge it as a principle that to speak of the question of *existence* in cases in which empirical verifiability is rejected in principle, is to utter the meaningless. It may perhaps be instructive to relate this objection, which involves an application of a more general theory of meaning, to the scientific situation which actually has provided the latter with some formidable support.

The physicist, when explaining the theory of relativity, sometimes says that 'there is no meaning in absolute motion'.[1] By absolute motion we understand the motion of a physical system with respect, not to some other body, but to empty space. Now to say that the concept of such a motion is meaningless is to say that no physical experiments could conceivably inform us of its existence. 'Conceivably', because such information would be in conflict with the principle of relativity. This principle amounts to the statement that physical laws refer indiscriminately to any system moving with uniform relative velocity. And so we have the statement,

[1] H. Dingle, *The Special Theory of Relativity*, 1940, p. 1.

'Absolute motion cannot be verified or falsified; therefore, this concept of motion is meaningless'. Here, the idea that absolute motion is meaningless connects with something positive, for it serves as an indirect reference to a physical law, viz. the principle of relativity. But with this compare : 'The existence of scientific entities cannot be verified or falsified by science; therefore, this concept of existence is meaningless'. Now the ascription of meaninglessness does *not* refer us back to anything positive. Rather it draws our attention to a peculiarity in a certain type of assertion, to a peculiar *use* of expression. It does not so much *refute* the metaphysical assertion as proscribe it.

These considerations show that the verificationist argument is not decisive against a metaphysical position. Still, at the same time, they illustrate its very peculiarity. True, it is now immune from criticism both on the grounds of truth as well as meaning. Yet, only at a price. For has not now the metaphysical assertion abandoned all claim to real effectiveness and to any sort of relevance to concrete issues? If so, what can be its purpose? Let us retrace the steps which led to this situation. Within science there is a fairly well though not rigidly circumscribed way in which we think of both evidence for and conclusion to the existence of certain things, *e.g.* a fixed electric charge carried by an electron, and (less clearly) an electron. But reflection on the indirectness (rather than incompleteness) and theoretical nature of the evidence produces an uneasiness. This may be expressed by rejecting the normal relations which we usually feel to hold between evidence and conclusion. This uneasiness is reflected as well as aggravated by a temptation to adopt a certain *model* of existence or reality as a standard to which all else must approximate on pain of being dubbed 'mere appearance'. Mach's objects of sense and instantial cases are such models. Of course, as I suggested, there must be something essentially arbitrary about the metaphysical assertion that these are the right models. This arbitrariness is reflected in the fact that they are not open to empirical criticism.

Let me clarify and reinforce this by looking at the second type of puzzle situation, connected with the status of scientific laws in general.

III

Consider once more Mach's statement, 'In nature there is no *law* of refraction, there are only individual cases of refraction'. Is this not very paradoxical? It sounds as though we had no evidence for the existence of laws at all. Yet would one not want to say that we had every evidence? Well, there *are* answers to this, answers which hint at a more fundamental sort of doubt. For instance, can one be *absolutely* certain that some individual law or theory will cover the future state of the world? Perhaps you will reply that in the eventuality of finding a certain law no longer applicable we shall modify or replace it by an improved formulation. You will be told that these considerations are irrelevant. For in the first place you have no warrant to assume that what we have learnt will be of the slightest consequence when it comes to anticipating the future. And as for abandoning a law which is found to be inadequate, the question was really whether we were justified to put forward any law in the first place. In this way Max Planck, the founder of the first Quantum theory, in his *The Universe in the Light of Modern Physics*, said:

> We have no right to assume that any physical laws exist, or if they have existed up to now, that they will continue to exist in a similar manner in the future.[1]

You will notice that though all this sounds like coming from someone who is simply telling you to be careful about the conclusions one is to draw from our experiments, there must be something more that is at stake. I am not saying that there is no problem; only, that if there is one there is absolutely nothing in our experience or in the organized body of science that would be allowed to have the slightest bearing on its solution. Max Born, another physicist, echoed this when he wrote recently that a solution would be a 'question of faith', and any formal statement of a principle offering one, 'a metaphysical principle'.[2]

A doubt when pressed in this way I shall therefore call a metaphysical doubt. What is the source of this abandonment of the empirical field and of the passage to a doubt that has no limit? Suppose you said that the discovery of so many scientific facts and laws surely ought to constitute *some* bona-fide consideration in favour of saying that there are laws. Well, I think that Mach's idea mentioned before

---

[1] M. Planck, *The Universe in the Light of Modern Physics*, 1931, p. 63.
[2] M. Born, *The Natural Philosophy of Law and Chance*, 1949, p. 7.

would suggest a possible answer. 'Though there are what scientists *call* "laws *of nature*" ', he would say, 'there are no laws *in nature*.' Once again, Mach seems to have some special criterion by which to judge this question and some quite separate aims in coming to his conclusion. This is suggested by his shifting from the expression 'law of nature', which raises no problems, to the far more debatable one, 'law in nature'.

To expand what I said about the previous example, I think that to deny the existence of 'laws in nature' is to assert that what are *called* 'laws' do not come up to some particular standard of reality and that to the concept of law there does not correspond anything sufficiently fundamental. 'Not coming up to a certain standard of reality' means that in some essential aspects a law is unlike something (which I will call an 'empirical analogue') that does (or is asserted to) satisfy such a standard. (In this account the term 'reality' must necessarily remain undefined.) Thus, for Mach, whatever is an element of direct sensation, or at any rate, an 'individual case', would satisfy. Now, of course, laws *are* logically different from their instances; were they to usurp the essential features of instances they would cease to be laws; yet, unless they do so (Mach's argument implies) they must be rejected.

It will be seen then that by sharpening certain distinctions and allowing one of the things distinguished a place of pre-eminence, metaphysical positions are built up which through their very paradoxical formulations shock us into reconsidering continually the difficulties that produce them. Considered in this way they are natural though perhaps not inevitable outgrowths of our reasonings.

IV

This will explain what lies at the back of the metaphysician's attitude of rejection and the nature of his unlimited doubt. How well Hume illustrated this when in his *History of England* he wrote :

> While Newton seemed to draw off the veil from some of the mysteries of nature, he shewed at the same time the imperfections of the mechanical philosophy; and thereby restored her ultimate secrets to that obscurity, in which they ever did and ever will remain.[1]

Here we find limitless doubt with respect to the results of scientific theorizing in general, a doubt which involves the third and last of our puzzle situations.

I said that we must think of a theory as more than something merely connecting known facts and laws in a systematic way. For the major scientific theories are meant to give us a deeper understanding; they connect a number of facts which without them would remain quite loose and separate. Moreover, a theory gives these facts added support. But questions arise again. How could theoretical connectives such as the forces of dynamics support phenomena which already rest on the strongest possible foundation, namely observation and experiment? Again, if theories are to tell us how and why things essentially connect, how could this be effected by supplying us

[1] D. Hume, *The History of England*, 1773, vol. 8, p. 332.

with further facts which in principle must lack the sort of connection that was felt to be missing in the original set?

Although I have put my questions very crudely in order to bring out more clearly the genesis of a metaphysical position it should be realized that even a more careful treatment would reveal some real difficulties. One example will have to be sufficient. Consider Newton's theory of gravitation. Newton had explained certain uniformities of planetary motion by deriving them from a few simple laws of nature, the so-called laws of motion, together with the law of gravitation which involved the hypothesis of a universal attractive force acting between sun and planets across empty space. It was at this point that certain fundamental objections came to be raised. Berkeley, for instance, complains that this theory is not *really* an explanation, for, granted that the original facts to be explained were nothing more than brute facts (lacking all essential connection), so were the explaining laws which (as he says) were not more than

rules . . . observed in the productions of natural effects, the efficient and final causes whereof are not of mechanical consideration.[1]

But, you may ask, doesn't Newton postulate something like an efficient cause, namely, his attractive force? Berkeley had his answer ready, saying that we cannot be

concerned at all about forces, neither can we know or measure them otherwise than by their effects, that is to

[1] G. Berkeley, *Works*, ed. Fraser, vol. 3, *Siris*, sect. 231.

say, the motions. . . . What is said of forces residing in bodies, whether attracting or repelling, is to be regarded only as a mathematical hypothesis, and not as any thing really existing in nature.[1]

Ominous phrase, this last one! Of course, I am not suggesting that there were no difficulties in Newton's conceptions of force and mass, space and time ; and these criticisms were not the least of the factors that have contributed to the revolution in science during the present century. Also, Berkeley was quite correct to point out that Newton's 'mechanical principles' were insufficient to account for 'numberless other effects', *e.g.* chemical and electrical ones. What is interesting to us is to see how this empirical critique is inextricably mixed up with a metaphysical prudishness which, whilst acting as a sort of psychological stimulus on the former, ultimately would reject almost any normal explanation of natural processes as not sufficiently ultimate. Newton himself, partly under pressure from the side of Leibniz, had admitted that gravitational attraction at a distance ought to be explained in terms of something involving a medium which allowed of contiguous action. Berkeley would not accept this as an explanation of motions, since (as he says) 'the elasticity of one uniform medium . . . is not less obscure'.[2] Why 'obscure'? The answer is clear :

Nothing mechanical is or really can be a cause. [Anything that is a force cannot be] discovered by experiments or mathematical reasonings, which reach no farther than discernible effects, and motions in things

[1] *Ibid.* sect. 234. [2] *Ibid.* sect. 243.

77

passive and moved. . . . What these 'forces' are, which are supposed to be . . . impressed on bodies . . . hath been found very difficult, not to say impossible, for thinking men to conceive and explain.[1]

I think it will be agreed that behind this criticism there lurks a refusal to accept what is offered because Berkeley is troubled by the problem of explanation in general. And this is reflected in the adoption of yet another empirical model or analogue, namely mind or spirit. It is mind alone which can connect and act as an efficient cause, a doctrine which Berkeley thought was supported by the reflection that it is *in* our minds that we can most perfectly discover the right analogue of causation; as when we *imagine* ourselves as pushing or lifting an object.

We cannot make even one single step in accounting for the phenomena, without admitting the immediate presence and . . . action of an incorporeal agent, who connects, moves and disposes all things according to such rules . . . as seem good to him.[2]

There is no need here to criticize this notion in any detail. It clearly operates as a closure to an unlimited doubt, itself in turn fed by the adoption of this particular analogue, mind.

We see then through these examples how metaphysical doctrines connect with difficulties that arise out of a reflection on the logical procedures of science. Though scientific concepts, laws and theories must be considered as the natural foundation underlying the phenomena of our experienced world, as soon as we reflect we are tempted to say that the relation

[1] G. Berkeley, *op. cit.* sects. 247, 249.   [2] *Ibid.* sect. 237.

of dependence must be inverted. Laws certainly have to be dug out piecemeal; one cannot speak of observing and experiencing them as one does of the results of an experimental set-up or of the instruments used to that purpose. There is a further complication. Many of the chief scientific principles exhibit features which make them look more like methodological procedural rules through which we agree to describe nature; witness, Newton's laws of motion; the principle of conservation of energy; the principle of relativity; and so on. Remembering this we are tempted to conclude (as Eddington did [1]) that instead of giving us *a posteriori* knowledge derived by study of the *results* of observation, such laws give us *a priori* knowledge derived by epistemological study of the *procedure* of observation; that laws are not 'in nature' but are 'things of the thought' (Mach).

And yet, so we want to ask, is it not just as certain that we *observe*, or at any rate, *discover*, the orderliness and lawfulness of nature that prevails all around us? And so we get the puzzle: Shall we say that we discover and observe it or that we do not? That it is in nature or that it is not? One may describe this as a mere dispute as to what to *say* about certain definite empirical situations. Only, we should remember that we are not in possession of any *rules* which would tell us what to say. And so insensibly we are driven to take our stand somewhere. Whilst we do not take it arbitrarily, the choice is not straightforwardly a matter of science or logic. Mach's own position vitally affected his criticism of contemporary physical theory leading him to a reappraisal of the

[1] A. Eddington, *The Philosophy of Physical Science*, 1939, p. 24.

status of laws and theories but in particular to a criticism of the Newtonian definitions of mass, force, absolute space and time ; in each case pointing out that those definitions did not lead to clear empirical procedures and hence lacked operational significance. Forces he rejected because they failed to have the logical features of elements of sensation and thus were not sufficiently ultimate.

This is interesting. For strangely enough, Berkeley rejected them almost for the same reason. Yet he was unwilling to interpret explanations solely in terms of observable phenomena, atomistically conceived elements of sensation. The ideal theory was for him something more ultimate, something *not* reducible to statements about rules ordering the phenomena. He looked for an 'efficient cause', as he terms it, for connectives which really connect. Hence his doctrine of universal mind-like connection. Thus, where Berkeley rejects Newtonian forces because they are not sufficiently like what he would admit as coming up to the ideal of substantial *connectives*, Mach rejects them because they are not sufficiently like substantial *elements*. The logical bond between metaphysical axiom and empirical principle is evidently not very close. Yet undoubtedly in both cases metaphysical preferences performed the important function of making these thinkers more conscious of the nature of the physical theories involved.

v

We meet, however, on occasion with expressions of metaphysical preferences which have exerted a somewhat more direct and positive influence on the development of scientific thought. They may direct the search for specific types of scientific laws of a certain form. I will mention just one example.

We found Berkeley suggest that true explanations should exhibit some sort of end or purpose. Years earlier Leibniz had said that it was an important characteristic of reality that — like a mathematical or scientific system — it exhibits 'the greatest simplicity in hypotheses and the greatest wealth in phenomena'.[1] More specifically, everything in nature seemed to 'turn on considerations of greatest and least'.[2] This was an oblique reference to a certain minimum principle which Leibniz, following Fermat, had found useful in an application to the problems of geometrical optics. The principle involved an assertion that in nature certain quantities (at first only defined very vaguely) are always minimized. Developments of this idea have subsequently led to elegant unifications of dynamical, optical and electro-dynamical theory. Now it is clear that for Leibniz minimum principles played the important rôle of what I have called 'empirical analogues'. It was as such that in his hands and those of later writers from Maupertuis to Helmholtz and Planck, action principles seemed to possess such powerful explanatory force. The subsequent discovery that these principles were merely alternative mathematical expressions of facts which could be

---

[1] G. W. Leibniz, *On the Ultimate Origination of Things*, ed. Everyman, 1934, p. 34.

[2] Leibniz, *Discourse on Metaphysics*, ed. Lucas and Grant, 1953, sect. 6, p. 10.

rendered by equations descriptive of the usual 'mechanical causation' type; and that furthermore they were not always 'minimum' principles but might involve a 'maximum' instead, does not in the least detract from the *significance* of the original metaphysical views built round them though, of course, it does considerably change our ideas of their *status*.

Wittgenstein characterized the situation in an interesting fashion when he wrote in his *Tractatus* that 'Men had indeed an idea that there must be *a* "law of least action" before they knew exactly how it ran'; [1] and that it was in this sense that we may say that they possessed *a priori* knowledge, at least of the possibility of a law of a certain form. You see, we want to say, not just that we have the best possible evidence for *believing* in such laws; we want to say that we *know* they are fundamental. It is through metaphysics that men attempt to give a logical sense to this requirement.

[1] L. Wittgenstein, *Tractatus Logico-Philosophicus*, 1933, sects. 6.3211, 6.33, 6.34.

METAPHYSICS AND HISTORY

WE are all familiar with questions like 'Who won the battle of Waterloo?' and 'What were the causes of the English Civil War?' Questions like these are questions about what happened to, and what was done by, particular human beings at particular times, and why; they can only be settled by appeals to evidence and sources; and the business of answering them belongs, in the first instance, to historians.

But there are, of course, other kinds of questions which may be asked about history. We may, for instance, want to consider the ways in which historians are accustomed to discuss and settle questions of the sort I have just mentioned; thus we may ask how they select and interpret the evidence at their disposal, or what types of argument they use to establish their conclusions; again, we may be interested in what they mean, to what they are committed, by some of the things they say. These are questions of method and logic, and their subject-matter is, not history considered as what happened, but history considered as what historians do and say when they try to make out and describe what happened.

Sometimes, however, we find a third type of question raised. Questions of this sort are not about particular historical events, nor are they about historical procedure; instead they refer to the historical process as a whole. And so we sometimes find people enquiring whether history in general has any goal or meaning or purpose; whether it presents a coherent pattern or rhythm; whether there are universal laws governing its direction and development; whether it 'makes sense'. It is questions of this kind which have tended to give rise to metaphysical theories of history, and it will therefore be with them, and with the answers they have provoked, that I shall chiefly be concerned in this essay.

It would be wrong, however, to suppose that *all* questions asked about the historical process as a whole lead into metaphysics. For some theories of history are set out in terms which suggest that they are meant to be interpreted empirically; that is to say, what they assert appears to be grounded upon, and to be checked against, historical facts as these are known to us through the writings of historians. The theory may, for instance, aim to show that the course history has so far followed represents a certain trend — a trend, perhaps, towards increasing technical control over nature, or towards greater intellectual and spiritual enlightenment, or, again, towards the realization of some political ideal, like the ideal of individual liberty. Views of this kind were put forward by a number of eighteenth- and nineteenth-century writers — Condorcet and Herbert Spencer are examples. Again, a modern historical theory of the type to be found in Professor Toynbee's *A Study of History* may state laws which (it is claimed) can be seen to determine the growth and decay of civilizations. Professor Toynbee describes his method as 'inductive', by which he means that the laws he formulates have been suggested and confirmed by an intensive examination of the behaviour of different cultures. Whether the procedure he adopts is an acceptable one and whether his practice is always consistent with his principles, are, of course, separate problems; the point is that his theory is at any rate *put forward* as an empirical one, subject to the tests of observed fact and to these alone.

What, then, distinguishes metaphysical interpretations of history from ones like these? Let us begin by considering an example, a fairly simple one. Kant thought that history offered a challenge, a challenge that might be put in the form of the question: 'To what rational plan does history, viewed as a single process, conform?' And he believed that a clue to the answer to this question could be found by considering the human character. For, if we do this, we shall see that certain capacities have, in his words, been 'implanted by Nature' in human beings, capacities which are, he says, 'destined to unfold themselves completely and conformably to their end in the course of time'. Thus history must be viewed as moving according to 'a plan of Nature' towards the realization of these innate capacities, and Kant held that the course history has pursued to date in fact bears out this interpretation.

Now it is important to notice that Kant seems to be claiming to do more than merely detect an actual trend in the development of history. For he seems also to be suggesting, first, that it was *necessary* that this trend should have been what it has been, and, secondly, that he can explain *why* it was necessary. Nevertheless, the explanation he provides is of a peculiar kind.

To show how it is peculiar, consider the ways in which we sometimes explain happenings in terms of the plans or policies of intelligent agents. Kant speaks as if what he calls 'Nature' were such an agent, and as if what he regards Nature as having done could furnish us with evidence about her plans for the human species. And the type of explanation to which he appears to appeal is one to which we might well appeal if we were asked why it was, for instance, that certain plants were to be found growing in a particular flower-bed. In this case it might be said that they had been put there by a gardener, and that the gardener's purpose in doing so was that they should in due course blossom as peonies. But there are important points at which this explanation is unlike the one Kant gives us. For, to begin with, it relies upon empirical knowledge of a number of facts — the existence of gardeners whose habits and activities are familiar to us through observation and experience, for example — and we can find no parallel to this in Kant's mysterious references to Nature and her alleged aims. Further, whereas it makes sense to ask whether or not the gardener's purposes were fulfilled by what happened to the flowers, since we can compare what he set out to do with what he actually achieved, there is no conceivable way of tracking down Nature's plans for the development of the human species apart from noticing how human capacities and talents have in fact been realized in the course of history. And, if this is so, then what Kant says about history having necessarily occurred as it has occurred, because it has been 'ordained' or 'planned' that it should, begins to look less impressive. His 'explanation' seems to come to little more than a restatement of the facts it was introduced to explain — he has described them in unusual language, calling them 'the realization of Nature's intentions'.

Kant himself was by no means unaware of some of these points. He did not, for example, believe that he had *proved* that his interpretation of history was correct: he did not, indeed, think that any speculations of this sort *could* be proved. But other philosophers have been less circumspect. And many metaphysical theories about history owe their appeal and fascination to the fact that they have seemed capable of justifying, by familiar and accepted methods, startling conclusions concerning the nature of the historical process. We are told, not merely that history has, as a matter of fact, taken a certain course, but that it *had* to take this course. Moreover, the metaphysician's ability to explain the past as a necessary development has often been thought to equip him to predict the future also. And with this comes the view that history is the product of relentless unobservable 'forces', whose behaviour we can admire or regret (as the case may be), but whose operations we cannot change or withstand.

But, even if the interpretations of history which metaphysicians offer do not provide us, as they seem to do, with new facts, but rather with new ways of describing old facts, we have still to ask why they have been put forward. In the case of Kant the answer is not difficult to find. For, if we describe history as conforming to a purpose, then it becomes possible to discuss it in moral terms; and this was something Kant was anxious that we should be able to do. What happens in history, Kant implied, can only be justified if the course of history is the expression of a plan, a plan which has as its objective a morally desirable state of affairs. And such notions as that history proceeds according to moral laws, or that it is the embodiment of justice, meting out rewards and punishments to those who recognize or fail to recognize its authority, are ones that have proved as comforting to metaphysicians eager to recommend particular ethical and political creeds as they have proved useful to politicians and propagandists with less exalted aims.

There is, however, something else to be noticed about theories of the kind we are considering. In the Introduction to these essays, it was pointed out that it is a characteristic of metaphysics to extend certain selected ideas and concepts beyond the spheres within which they are normally used. And the metaphysician's open dissatisfaction with many of the beliefs we ordinarily accept — whether these be the beliefs of common sense, or the statements and hypotheses of science or history — can, in part at least, be traced back to their not having been shown to conform as a whole to some preferred pattern of description or interpretation. Thus Descartes, admiring the certainty and power of mathematical reasoning and proof, demanded that our knowledge of nature should be expressed in the form of a rigorous deductive system founded upon premisses which are self-evident and indubitable. And similarly various philosophers have argued that it is not enough, in the case of history, merely to bring to light the connections that link together particular events and circumstances; it is not even enough to show that they illustrate, or form part of, an overall tendency or trend visible in the course of history in general. More must be done. And these philosophers, taking some chosen model of interpretation — for example, the purposive type of explanation where the actions of an individual person are treated as the expression of a policy or plan — have insisted that the historical process as a whole must, if it is to be understood at all, be understood in terms of this model. Only in this way can the vast number of separate events, which are discussed so glibly by historians, be shown to form a satisfying and intelligible unity.

Now the belief that, fully to explain something, it is necessary to present it as having a purpose or as conforming to a plan is, of course, very old and deep-seated, and the application of such ideas to the course of history *in toto* need not surprise us. On the other hand, I think it is also worth noticing that explanations of this kind are ones that tend to play a central rôle in the *ordinary* writing of history, when it is the behaviour of particular persons in particular circumstances that is in question. For philosophical interest in history came to the fore in the late eighteenth and early nineteenth centuries, at a time when historical studies were gaining a new significance and developing in fresh and unexpected directions; and it would, therefore, be natural to find philosophers, impressed by these advances, assigning an important place to the sorts of explanation historians are accustomed to use. And this is, in fact, what we do find. Thus we discover them, not only employing typically historical ideas as the key to their interpretations of the entire historical process, but treating them also as the key to their interpretations of reality in general. In this way historical metaphysics may emerge at two different levels. On the first level it appears as an attempt to explain or order the *whole* of history in terms of an idea normally used to explain particular events occurring *within* history — the idea, for example, of a plan. On the second level, it appears as an attempt to interpret the whole of *reality* in the light of such an idea. And from these more extended theories of reality, theories of the first kind — interpretations, that is, of the historical process — are thought to follow as necessary consequences.

Hegel, for example, certainly had a theory of the why and wherefore of the historical process. But his 'philosophy of history' formed only a part, although an essential part, of a far wider system that included the philosophies of mind and nature. This system is very elaborate, and it conforms closely to the programme which another German philosopher, Schopenhauer, claimed to be the only possible one for philosophy, the programme of providing 'a complete and accurate . . . expression of the nature of the world in very general concepts'. And what makes Hegel's system interesting, from our point of view, is that the 'very general concepts' lying at its centre are ideas of an historical kind.

How is Hegel's picture of the world best described? Perhaps it can be most conveniently considered by contrasting it with other metaphysical systems which have been inspired, not by history, but by mathematics and science. Hegel called mathematics a 'defective kind of knowledge', and he thought that its influence upon philosophy had been disastrous. Why?

He believed, in the first place, that mathematics assumes the validity of such basic logical laws as that a thing cannot be what it is not and must be what it is. But, on Hegel's view, the world does not conform 'in its essence' to these laws: they do not represent the final truth of things. And so, while he did not want to deny that mathematics has its legitimate uses, he considered previous philosophers to have been totally mistaken in treating it as a model to which all our knowledge of the world should conform.

But what of the remarkable claim upon which this contention is founded — the claim that the traditional laws of logic are in some way untrue to the innermost character of the world: in Hegelian terminology, that reality is ultimately 'contradictory'? Although I think that it involves a number of different ideas, part of its meaning can perhaps be brought out by taking into account the notion of *change*. When things change or alter they are different at one moment from what they are at the next. Now it does not, of course, by any means follow from the fact that we describe a changing thing differently at different times that we are contradicting ourselves: still less, that the thing itself is contradictory. But metaphysicians are seldom inhibited by considerations of this kind. And I think we can interpret Hegel as expressing, in a very misleading fashion, a view of the world according to which everything is seen as subject to constant movement, fluctuation and shift. Truly to understand it we must regard it, not as something fixed and static, but as a continuous process or course of development. Thus Engels attributed to Hegel what he called 'the great basic thought that the world is not to be comprehended as a complex of ready-made *things*, but as a complex of *processes*'.

Hegel, however, undertook to show that a concentration of attention upon mathematics was dangerous in another way to philosophy. For to use mathematics to talk about the world — as, for example, physicists do — is to take into account only those characteristics of things which are capable of measurement — their size, weight and so forth. In other words, it is to regard them from a purely quantitative point of view. And philosophers like Descartes, reflecting this approach, argued that extension or size constituted the essence of things. According to Hegel, on the other hand, quantity is precisely what is *not* essential.

What were the reasons for this belief? Hegel's philosophy is dominated by the conviction that reality is, in the last resort, not material but mental. It must, therefore, be mistaken (on this view) to suppose that a concept like that of quantity applies to the world in its innermost, or 'real', nature. For it is only in place to speak of size or weight when we are talking of *matter* ; we cannot, for example, talk in any literal sense of measuring thoughts or of weighing ideas. Yet it is precisely in terms of the notions of *thought* or *idea* that, according to Hegel, the true structure of reality must be understood and explained. And so, when he spoke of the world as a process, the sort of process he had in mind was a process of a specific type. It was not a 'blind' or unconscious process of the sort exhibited by the behaviour of certain natural phenomena — the growth of plants, for example : his model was rather that of a train of thought or argument, each stage of which develops from, or rises out of, what has gone before. And this caused him to claim that the world must be regarded as the expression of an evolving idea or mind ; it is a rational, self-determining system, perpetually moving forward according to its own inner laws.

Hegel's metaphysics, then, turns out to be dominated by two main conceptions — the thought of reality as a developing process, and the thought of reality as inherently rational. And although these conceptions may at first sight seem strange, they can, I think, be made to look less curious, or at any rate more understandable, if we consider them in the light of certain aspects of historical explanation. Hegel, for instance, wishes us to believe that, in order to understand anything, it is necessary to see it as part of a rational process. And a historian, when he wants to make a particular happening or circumstance intelligible, often tries to show how it fitted into, or formed part of, or illustrated, some more general movement or trend or pattern. In this way, interpretation or explanation by reference to processes of development represents a notable part of the historian's method. Nor is this all. It has often, for example, been claimed that what distinguishes the human studies in general, and history in particular, from other types of knowledge lies in the fact that their subject-matter is of a special kind. For the occurrences with which they deal are essentially the product or expression of thoughts, policies, motives and the like; and this is not true of the events studied, for example, by a physicist or a chemist. The historian is, therefore, able to understand and interpret his subject-matter in a peculiarly intimate way. For he can 'get inside' his characters, and, by putting himself in their position and state of mind, see what they are up to.

Thus, from this point of view, what Hegel says can be seen to reflect two important features of historical writing. Only the reflection is of a curious — and, one might add, typically metaphysical — kind. For Hegel is claiming that reality in general — not merely events as they are discussed by historians — must be described and explained in terms of processes of development. And he is claiming that reality in general — not merely human activities and behaviour — must be seen as the expression of a rational mind. In other words, according to him, knowing reality for what it 'really' is consists in understanding the rational principles governing its movement, and this we can do because we are ourselves rational beings. Thought corresponds to reality because reality is thought.

I am suggesting, then, that we can consider a

metaphysical system like Hegel's as underlining — in a peculiar way — certain familiar characteristics of historical writing and method. But I think such theories have also a more constructive function.

First, it is worth pointing out that theories of this type don't merely *reflect* — they also *select*. We have seen, for instance, that Hegel gave priority of place to explanations of a kind often used by historians. But they also use different kinds. And other historical theorists — notably Marx — have emphasized the importance of these. Marx and Engels did not, it is true, work out a coherent system in the Hegelian sense; but they took over many of Hegel's principal ideas. For them, however, (unlike Hegel), the basic conception in terms of which everything must ultimately be interpreted and explained was the conception, not of mind, but of matter. And, in treating 'matter' as their fundamental idea, they were influenced, not by explanations which refer to intentions or thoughts or plans in people's heads, but by explanations which refer to 'external' *causes*, operating upon them from without and determining what they do.

Now, to emphasize one type of explanation which historians use at the expense of another which they also use is to express a preference. And, having made a choice in favour of causal as contrasted with purposive explanations, Marx went on to make a further choice concerning the relative significance of different *sorts* of causes. The ultimately decisive factors in historical change were (he thought) technical and economic factors, such as advances in the methods men use in order to produce what satisfies their needs, and the class antagonisms and conflicts resulting from these. So when he came to explain the rise of Napoleon III to power in France, Marx chiefly concerned himself, not with the ideas and stated aims of those who took part in this event, but with the economic condition and class-structure of France at the time, which, he believed, 'in the last analysis' determined their behaviour. Marx may therefore be regarded as putting forward proposals as to how history should be done. These proposals have without any doubt had a far-reaching effect upon the approach of historians to their subject and they can be considered without taking into account the more sensational aspects of the materialist conception of history. But at this point the line between the metaphysical and the empirical elements in Marx's theory becomes difficult to draw. For, presumably, the fruitfulness of Marx's recommendations can only be judged by trying them out; and this is an empirical matter. On the other hand we may be told, in cases where the proposed method does not seem to fit, or appears even to be a positive obstruction, that there really do exist 'deeper' economic causes for which the only evidence is a theory claiming that they 'must' exist. And then we may legitimately feel suspicious that what is being said does not concern a genuine question of fact.

Another way in which historical metaphysics may prove fertile is this. By constructing systems which involve extending the meaning of certain familiar words, by putting old terms to new and wider uses, metaphysicians have sometimes suggested fresh methods of describing and ordering the material of history. One may instance Hegel's employment of the word 'principle' in this connection. Hegel spoke as if each stage in the process of rational development that constitutes the world were governed by a principle; and he applied his idea to human history, which is part of this process, in an interesting way. For to each phase of the history of mankind Hegel assigns a particular principle which, he says, 'defines the common features of its religion, its political constitution, its morality, its system of law, its *mores*, even of science, art and technical skill'. In saying this, he was expressing the idea that there are close connections and likenesses between the different manifestations of cultural life at a particular period, and that it is often helpful to interpret a historical age or epoch in the light of some single leading conception. And the belief that various periods of history can be described in relation to certain very general ideas, such as 'Protestantism', or 'liberalism', or 'capitalism' — that we can even regard them as being in some sense the 'expression' of these — is one that has struck deep roots in the minds of many historians, from Ranke to the present day. Even if Hegel was not the originator of this view, he was one of the first to make it articulate.

In conclusion, then, we might think of metaphysical theories of history as being in some respects like diagrams. Diagrams do not represent things as they are in reality: they throw certain features into relief and exclude others. And historical metaphysicians offer us a kind of diagrammatic picture in which only certain conceptions and ideas appear.

Like diagrams, their theories may be illuminating and
suggestive. But, treated as what they claim to be —
comprehensive representations from which nothing
is left out and where all is accounted for — they
may lead us into bewilderment, or mislead us into
nonsense.

METAPHYSICS AND ETHICS

What should a philosophical study of morals be like? This is a question concerning which there is a certain amount of doubt among modern philosophers. When I speak about modern philosophers and modern philosophy I shall be meaning that present-day version of our traditional empiricism which is known as linguistic analysis — and although a lot of what I have to say will be critical of recent developments in that tradition, the criticisms which I make will also come, I believe, out of the tradition. To understand current moral philosophy it is necessary to understand its history. And here it is convenient to begin from the moment when G. E. Moore made a certain distinction. Moore said we should distinguish between the question, what things are good? and the question, what does the word 'good' mean? On this second question Moore had important things to say. He claimed that 'good' was indefinable, and that previous moral philosophers, because they had failed to distinguish those two questions from each other, had fallen into the error of defining 'good', or 'valuable', in terms of some other non-valuable entity, whether a natural entity, such as pleasure, or a metaphysical entity, such as rationality. If asked, what *things* are good, one might indeed answer this

99

question by pointing to pleasure or to rationality — but one could not answer the question what is *good itself* in this way. Moore convinced his readers of this very simply by pointing out that it made *sense* always, given any proposition of the form 'X is good', to withdraw thoughtfully and ask — 'But is X really good?' That is, the notion of 'good' could significantly be attached to or withdrawn from anything whatever, and the things to which it happened to be attached did not form part of its meaning.

This simple argument of Moore's produced a complete change of perspective in moral philosophy. It transformed the central question of ethics from the question, 'What is goodness?' — where an answer was expected in terms of the revelation of some real and eternally present structure of the universe — into the question — 'What is the activity of "valuing" (or "commending")?', where what is required is to see what is in common to people of all ages and societies when they attach value to something. This phrase 'attach value' is itself significant of the change of attitude. The philosopher is now to speak no longer of the Good, as something real or transcendent, but to analyse the familiar human activity of endowing things with value. If we want to place the definitive breach with metaphysical ethics at any point, we can place it here.

Moore himself, however, was not wholly of the modern time in that although he pointed out that 'good' was not the second name of any other natural or metaphysical property, he could not rid himself of the conviction that it was nevertheless the name of *a* property, the unanalysable non-natural property of goodness, which inhered in certain actual states of affairs — so that although any proposition of the form 'X is good' could *make sense*, such a proposition would only be *true* if X really possessed the property of goodness.

Philosophers after Moore retained Moore's distinction of the two questions, and Moore's linguistic approach. They took it that the central question of ethics was the question 'What does "good" *mean*?' — but they refrained from answering the question 'What things are good?' and made it clear that this was a matter for the moralist, and not for the philosopher. Concerning the meaning of 'good', things then moved fast. What is known as the verificationist view of meaning, entering philosophy from the side of natural science, made a violent impact upon ethics. If the meaning of a proposition is the method of its verification, and if verification has to be in terms of observation of sensible events, then clearly ethical propositions could not have meaning in this way — and it was no use appealing to a mysterious property, not open to ordinary observation, to give them significance. Moore's non-natural property disappeared, in this more sceptical atmosphere, together with many other would-be metaphysical entities. Ethical propositions were clearly and firmly separated from other types of propositions and have remained so ever since. They were not, it was claimed, true or false, they did not state facts: they did not state *natural* facts, for the reason that Moore had given, and they did not state *metaphysical* facts, for the same reason, and also because there were none to state. It was then said that ethical propositions expressed emotion. They did not have *descriptive*, or factual, meaning, they had *emotive* meaning.

The emotive theory of ethics was not created as the result of a patient scrutiny of ethical propositions. It arose largely as the by-product of a theory of meaning whose most proper application was in other fields. The emotive theory was overthrown partly by a return to common sense; it was felt that, surely, ethical statements must somehow be regarded as rational, defensible by argument and by reference to fact. Partly, the theory disappeared as a result of two other philosophical developments: first, the notion that meaning should be analysed not in terms of method of verification, but in terms of *use*, and second, what might roughly be summed up as 'the disappearance of the mind'.

The notion that the meaning of a word is its use — a notion which in other fields we may associate with the name of Wittgenstein — did, I think, arise independently in the field of ethics, as a development and refinement of the emotive theory. Ethical statements were now said, not to express emotion, but to evoke emotion and more generally to persuade.

This is the view which we find most fully explained by Stevenson in his book *Ethics and Language*. Hard upon this development, however, and associated with the same change in our conception of meaning, there followed the revolution in our attitude to psychological concepts. When we speak of 'the mind', it was now maintained, we are not speaking of a set of inner entities such as faculties and feelings, which are open to introspection, we are speaking of observable actions and patterns of behaviour. We learn and we apply mental concept words on the basis of what we can openly observe. This new view, which was made widely known by Professor Ryle's book *The Concept of the Mind*, had consequences for moral philosophy. Previously a moral statement had been said to express an *attitude*, where this was conceived of in terms of the speaker's feelings, and, possibly his wish to influence the hearer's feelings. Now, if a moral statement was said to express an attitude, this was to be analysed rather in terms of the speaker's conduct, and his intent to influence the hearer's conduct. Moral statements had been treated first as exclamations and then as persuasions — now they were called imperatives or prescriptions or rules.

To adopt this analysis had the technical advantage of allowing the philosopher to express the essence of morality in a purely logical manner, without reference to either metaphysical or psychological entities, and in such a way that the old dilemma about whether moral remarks were subjective or objective was completely resolved. If a moral remark is not really a statement but a rule, then it cannot be subjective or objective, or true or false either. In this way two objections were met which had been made to Moore's ethics : it was now shown in the analysis that moral judgments were essentially practical (answers to the question 'What shall I do ?') and not in any way factual. Whereas Moore had treated moral remarks as expressions of moral insight, not as instances of moral advice, and he had clung to the idea that they were still in some sense factual. The new analysis corrected both these points. There remained the question, concerning which Moore's view had also been far from satisfactory, of the *rationality* of ethical judgments. This was met by a further refinement of technique. The distinction between 'descriptive' meaning (meaning *via* reference to fact) and 'evaluative' meaning, as it was now called, which had previously been only a distinction made between types of proposition, was now pressed into the structure of individual moral words. The meaning of the word 'good', for instance, was to be divided into an evaluative and a descriptive part. The descriptive part would consist of reference to the facts in virtue of which the speaker called something valuable — and the evaluative part would consist of the prescription — 'choose this one'. In this way the analysis could allow that a moral judgment might be discussed and defended by stating of facts — without itself becoming a factual statement.

Thus in a complex way, and by the successive correction of a series of theories, we have reached our present position — and the discussion goes on. This present position has, I think, been most clearly expounded in Mr. R. M. Hare's book *The Language of Morals*, and may be summed up as follows. A man's morality is seen in his conduct and a moral statement is a prescription or rule uttered to guide a choice, and the descriptive meaning of the moral word which it contains is made specific by reference to factual criteria of application. That is, in a moral statement we quasi-command that a particular thing be done, and are ready to say in virtue of what facts it ought to be done. We are also ready, if our moral statement is sincere, to do it ourselves in the appropriate circumstances. I think it is fair to take Mr. Hare's book as expressing the current position, although his book is under attack in many quarters. Most of these attacks, in my view, are upon the details of Mr. Hare's analysis and not upon its deep assumptions. What these assumptions are I shall discuss shortly.

Now this piece of our philosophical history might be described as the elimination of metaphysics from ethics. We are certainly now presented with a stripped and empty scene. Morality is not explained in terms of metaphysical concepts such as the rational will, nor in terms of psychological concepts such as moral feelings. It is not pictured by the philosopher, nor defended by philosophical arguments, as being attached to any real natural or metaphysical structure. It is pictured without any transcendent background. It is presented simply in terms of exhortations and choices defended by reference to facts. Now what has happened here exactly, and what have we been let in for? Let us look more closely.

The present view emerges from a very finely knit complex of mutual supporting arguments. To unravel this complex a bit, I suggest that we distinguish three types of argument on which this view may be said to rest. These are: *first*, a general critical argument to the effect that there are no metaphysical entities, *second*, a special critical argument, to the effect that even if there were, we could not base an analysis of morality upon them since it is impossible to argue from *is* to *ought*, from facts to values. *Third*, there are arguments, involving an appeal to our experience of morality, which support the various details of the analysis — the notion of guiding a choice, arguing, referring to facts, judging a man by his conduct, and so on.

About the first argument, which I shall call 'the anti-metaphysical argument', I shall be very brief. The criticism of metaphysics, which was always a part of our own tradition, and which was made systematic by Kant, is an established aspect of modern philosophy and has unavoidable implications for ethics. This is not to say, of course, that great moral conceptions such as 'the rational will' are senseless or useless, but simply that they cannot be established by certain familiar types of philosophical argument. This is a point I shall return to later. I go on now to argument number two.

This argument, which I shall call 'the anti-naturalistic argument', to the effect that we cannot derive values from facts is the most important argument in modern moral philosophy — indeed it is almost the whole of modern moral philosophy. Now this argument, as it has appeared in recent years, has a certain complexity about it. It is sometimes presented as if it were the exposure of a logical fallacy. When Moore called argument from 'is' to 'ought' 'the Naturalistic Fallacy' he implied just this — and in Mr. Hare's book the central argument, which is this same argument, is expressed in logical terms. To reach an imperative conclusion we need at least one imperative premise. We may also be encouraged to think of the argument in this way because of its original very striking formulation by Hume — and because Moore's formulation of it, which has so much caught our imagination, was made *à propos* of an obviously fallacious argument by John Stuart Mill: that is, Mill's argument that what in fact is desired is *ipso facto* what ought to be desired.

Now if the anti-naturalistic argument is designed merely to point out that a statement of value cannot be derived directly, and with no further help, from an ordinary statement of fact, then perhaps it may be called the exposure of a logical fallacy. But the trouble is that arguments of the crudity of Mill's argument are fairly rare in moral philosophy. If we want *pure* examples of this type of argument we are more likely to find them in the work of psychologists and sociologists than in the work of moral philosophers. What the great moral philosophers, in the past, have usually been doing is something much more complicated. They present a total metaphysical picture of which ethics forms a part. The universe, including our own nature, is like *this*, they say. Now this picture may be attacked by argument number one — that is straight philosophical criticism designed to show that the philosopher in question is not able to establish, by the argument he uses, the structure that he describes. But it is not so clear (although Moore, for instance, seems to have thought that it was) that such a picture of the place of morality can always be attacked by the second argument, the anti-naturalistic argument. Now it may be said — but surely the anti-metaphysical argument settles the matter. If we cannot establish transcendent metaphysical structures by philosophical argument then such structures cannot be the basis of ethics. But this is not so clear. What the moral philosopher professes to do nowadays is to analyse the essence of *any* morality, to display the logic of *any* moral language. But what place the concept of the transcendent may have in the structure of a morality is something which is *not* entirely settled by either the anti-metaphysical argument, or by the anti-naturalistic argument in its purely logical form. This narrow form of the anti-naturalistic argument I shall call 'the logical argument'. These arguments only prove that we cannot picture morality as issuing directly from a *philosophically established* transcendent background, or from a factual background. But this is not yet to say that the notion of *belief* in the transcendent can have no place in a philosophical account of morality.

Why has it been so readily assumed that the stripped and behaviouristic account of morality which the modern philosopher gives is imposed on us by philosophical considerations? I think this is because the anti-metaphysical argument and the logical argument have been very closely connected in the minds of those who used them with a much more general and ambiguous dictum to this effect: you cannot attach morality to the substance of the world. And this dictum, which expresses the whole spirit of modern ethics, has been accorded a sort of logical dignity. But, why can morality not be thought of as attached to the substance of the world? Surely many people who are not philosophers, and who cannot be accused of using faulty arguments since they use no arguments, do think of their

morality in just this way? They think of it as continuous with some sort of larger structure of reality,
whether this be a religious structure, or a social or
historical one.

Now I suggest there is another type of answer to
the question, why not attach morality to the substance of the world? — and that is a moral answer.
If you do this you are in danger of making your
morality into a dogma, you are in danger of becoming intolerant of the values of others, and of ceasing
to reflect on your own values through taking them
too much for granted. In short, if you start to think
of morality as part of a general way of conceiving
the universe, as part of a larger conceptual framework, you may cease to be reflective and responsible
about it, you may begin to regard it as a sort of
fact. And as soon as you regard your moral system
as a sort of fact, and not as a set of values which
only exist through your own choices, your moral
conduct will degenerate. This fear of moral de-
generation through lack of reflexion is to be found in
many modern writers on ethics, notably in the work
of Mr. Hare, whose book I have already mentioned.
It is also to be found, more positively asserted, in
many existentialist writers — and it may be found,
at what I take to be one of its sources, in that great
pamphlet of Liberalism, Mill's *Essay on Liberty*.

Now *this* sort of objection to picturing morality as
part of a systematic understanding of the world is
of a quite different type from the other objections.
This is not a logical or philosophical objection, it is
a straight moral objection to the effect that certain
bad results follow in practice from thinking about

morality in a certain way. We may agree with this. But to say it is of course *not* to say that morality cannot under any circumstances be part of a general system of belief about how the world is, or about transcendent entities. It is *not* to say that anything which involves such beliefs is not a morality — it is merely to maintain that the holding of such beliefs is morally and socially dangerous.

I am suggesting that modern philosophers have tended to take their stripped, behaviouristic and non-conceptual picture of morality as the only possible picture because they have joined the anti-metaphysical argument and the logical argument to a *moral* argument of a different type — a moral argument which properly belongs in the propaganda of liberalism. Why has this happened? I think it is not difficult to see if we consider the amount of support which what I have briefly called the be-haviouristic view of morals can gain from a study of the actual morality of our own society. Of the three arguments which support the current view of morals, I have so far discussed the anti-metaphysical argument — and the anti-naturalistic argument, which I suggested should be divided into (*a*) a rather narrow logical argument, and (*b*) a much more general moral argument. I come now to the third argument, or group of arguments, the appeal to our general conception of what morality is like.

Now clearly, if this appeal is made with the morals of our own liberal society in mind, there is a great deal in the behaviouristic picture of morals which receives immediate confirmation. We, in our society, believe in judging a man's principles by his conduct, in reflecting upon our own values and respecting the values of others, in backing up our recommendations by reference to facts, in breaking down intuitive conclusions by argument, and so on. Our morality is, on the whole, conceptually simple. We approach the world armed with certain general values which we hold *simpliciter* and without the assistance of metaphysics or dogmatic theology — respect for freedom, for truth, and so on. We study the facts, and we make our choices in the light of the facts and our values. Our disagreements among ourselves concern the application of principles — our disagreements with other societies concern what principles to hold. There are, of course, persons and groups among us whose morality is *not* conceptually simple, but metaphysical and dogmatic (for instance, some Christians and all Communists) — but these people are in the minority. It is therefore the case that the logical formula presented by the modern moral philosopher is on the whole a satisfactory representation of the morality most commonly held in England. The simplest moral words ('good' and 'right') are selected for analysis, their meaning is divided into a descriptive and an evaluative part, the descriptive part representing the factual criteria, the evaluative part representing a recommendation. And once the largely empirical disagreements about application of principles and classification of cases have been cleared up, ultimate moral differences will show as differences of choice and recommendation in a common world of facts. What the modern moral philosopher has done is what metaphysicians in the past have always done. He has produced a model. Only it is not a model of any morality whatsoever. It is a model of his own morality.

I want now to proceed with my discussion and to attempt to say more exactly what I think the philosopher's attitude ought to be towards what I have rather vaguely called conceptual or metaphysical frameworks within which morality may be placed. In order to do this I want to distinguish three different questions. These three questions are: *One*, Is morality to be seen as essentially and by its nature centred on the individual, or as part of a general framework of reality which includes the individual? *Two*, What kinds of arguments could establish the existence of such a general framework? and *Three*, What should the method of the moral philosopher now be like? I shall consider them in order.

First — Is morality to be seen as essentially centred on the individual? Now our tradition of thought tends to take it for granted that morality must be self-contained; and we can also invoke here the patronage of Kant, who says that the moral will is autonomous, and that morality cannot be founded on anything but itself. But equally, if we can come out of the trees and see the wood for a moment, it is clear that this is only one type of view of morality — roughly a Protestant, and less roughly a Liberal, type of view. Kant himself is the source not only of this Liberal morality, but also of a modern version of its opposite, which I shall call, with an old name, Natural Law morality, and about which I shall have more to say in a moment.

If we consider our own assumptions here we may discover many ways in which our empiricist tradition goes with the view of the moral will as something essentially separate and autonomous. None of our philosophers, apart from the idealists, has presented any elaborately metaphysical view of ethics. This is not surprising. Ethics and epistemology are always very closely related, and if we want to understand our ethics we must look at our epistemology. I think the most important person here is Hume. It is from him more than anyone else that we have derived a philosophical tendency, which is still with us, to see the world in terms of contingently conjoined simples, to see it as a totality of ultimate simple facts which have no necessary connection with each other. In so far as we imagine that the world does contain necessities, and that real connections exist between these simple elements, this is merely the result of habit and custom, which are themselves the work of Nature. It is only in reflective moments that we can see the ultimately disjoined character of the world. It is habit which gives to us, according to Hume, both our objective material world, and our moral world. Moral attitudes are habits of sentiment built up in society, and they do not need, and cannot have, any greater sanction. Since Hume was conservative in morals and politics he had no objection to morality continuing to be a matter of habit. But since he was also the empiricist that he was, he presents this habit as covering up the world of disconnected facts that lies behind it. *This* is what reflection would discover, to the moral consciousness as to the scientific consciousness.

With this the stage is set for the history of ethics

in this country. We oscillate between habit and reflection — the conservative side stressing habit, the progressive side stressing reflection. But notice still how much there is in common. Reflection is not metaphysical speculation, it is return to the facts. Burke, who was a great defender of tradition as a basis of morals, did not argue from a systematic or metaphysical background; indeed a rejection of system was a part of his outlook. Tradition and custom were to be taken as facts, as present realities, which were to be respected as such. Our traditionalists have not been metaphysicians, and neither have our progressives. The ideals which have inspired our society have been utilitarian ideals. And the utilitarians, when they wished to break down habit and custom by reflection, did not refer us to any metaphysical structure, but referred us to certain simple values and, above all, back again to the facts. The oscillation between habit and reflection may be seen today in moral philosophy itself in the contrast between, for instance, Professor Ryle and Professor Oakeshott on the one hand, both of whom hold that morality is and ought only to be a matter of habit, and Mr. Weldon and Mr. Hare on the other, who hold that morality is a matter of studying the facts and then making a reflective choice.

So, I suggest that in answering the question concerning whether morality is to be centred on the individual, we have been influenced partly by our own moral outlook and partly by our philosophical empiricism into assuming that it is of the *essence* of morality to be centred in this way. Nothing, we tend to assume, can *contain* the individual, except possibly his habits and his tradition, and these are merely facts like other ones, and capable of being reflectively examined. But this is only one way, roughly a Protestant, liberal, empiricist, way, of conceiving morality. What I have called Natural Law moralists — Thomists, Hegelians, Marxists — and less reflective persons who are camp followers of these doctrines, see the matter in a quite different perspective. The individual is seen as held in a framework which transcends him, where what is important and valuable is the framework, and the individual only has importance, or even reality, in so far as he belongs to the framework.

We may notice here some points of contrast between the Natural Law view and the Liberal view. On the Liberal view we picture the individual as able to attain by reflection to complete consciousness of his situation. He is entirely free to choose and responsible for his choice. His morality is exhibited in his choice, whereby he shows which things he regards as valuable. The most systematic exposition of modern liberal morality is existentialism. Contrast the Natural Law picture. Here the individual is seen as moving tentatively *vis-à-vis* a reality which transcends him. To discover what is morally good is to discover that reality, and to become good is to integrate himself with it. He is ruled by laws which he can only partly understand. He is not fully conscious of what he is. His freedom is not an open freedom of choice in a clear situation ; it lies rather in an increasing knowledge of his own real being, and in the conduct which naturally springs from such knowledge.

I would emphasize here that the contrast which I am remarking is not just a contrast between two philosophies; it is a contrast between two types of moral outlook. And here it should be added that of course not everyone in our society holds the liberal view in a pure form. Indeed the man in the street, and this goes for most ordinary non-philosophical Christians, is often a sort of non-metaphysical objectivist. That is, he believes that moral values are real and fixed — that is why he is so scandalized by the emotivists and the existentialists — but he has no clear view of nature or of history which is to explain the fixing of the values — and in this respect of course he differs, for instance, from the Marxist.

The logical picture of morality, which our modern philosophy has presented us with, shows no awareness of the importance of the contrast of which I have been speaking. We have been led to adopt a method of describing morality in terms of which all moral agents are seen as inhabiting the same world of facts, and where we are unable to discriminate between different types of morality, except in terms of differences of act and choice. Whereas, I am arguing, it is possible for differences to exist also as total differences of moral vision and perspective. From the Liberal point of view it seems axiomatic that however grandiose the structure may be in terms of which a morality extends itself, the moral agent is responsible for endowing this totality with value. The Liberal concentrates his attention on the *point of discontinuity* between the chosen framework and the choosing agent — and it is this moment of discontinuity which the modern philosopher has tried to catch in a formula. But for the individual, whether he be a Marxist or a Christian, who takes up a Natural Law point of view the scene looks completely different. Here there is no axiom of discontinuity. The individual's choice is less important, and the interest may lie in adoration of the framework rather than in the details of conduct. And here if the Liberal philosopher just goes on insisting that the moral agent is totally free by definition and is responsible for endowing the framework with value, and that 'ought' cannot be derived from 'is', this merely results in a colossally important difference of outlook being left unanalysed.

I now pass on to the second question, what kind of argument can establish whether or not there exists a transcendent non-empirical framework within which morality is to find its place. Here I shall be brief. It seems fairly clear that much of the criticism of traditional metaphysics, which modern philosophy has made its task, must stand. In addition there is the task of criticizing types of modern quasi-philosophy or semi-scientific metaphysics which seek to present the human mind as enclosed within social, historical, or psychological frames. I have in mind a great variety of views deriving from a study of Marx, Freud, the behaviour of calculating machines, and so on. It is in the criticism of such views that the logical argument (you can't derive 'ought' from 'is') is most often properly in place. The task of philosophy here may be said to be the definition and re-definition of human freedom *vis-à-vis* the various forces which, it is argued by arguments which are often more philosophical than empirical, may be said to threaten it. A recent example in this kind of defensive negative criticism is Mr. Isaiah Berlin's lecture *Historical Inevitability*, in which, in accents which remind us of Kierkegaard's attacks on Hegel, he argues that the individual cannot be shown to be enclosed by any framework of inevitable laws. This definition of freedom, which it is so important for philosophy to concern itself with, is achieved partly by such negative criticism. Is it also to be achieved by more positive means? This leads me to the last and most difficult question.

It is not at all clear, to me at any rate, what sort of philosophical method should now be used in the study of morals and politics. It has been assumed by moral philosophers that they have to be descriptive analysts as well as critics, that is, that they are to produce some sort of positive philosophical characterization of morality; and it seems that this is a reasonable requirement. But how is it to be done? I think that the implications for ethics of doing philosophy by the linguistic method have not yet become entirely clear. Words are tricky things and must be handled with care. We must not be too impressed by them — on the other hand, we must take them seriously enough. I think philosophers were too impressed by words when they assumed that all that was needed to effect the change-over in ethics from the old to the new régime was to put the word 'good' in inverted commas. The analysis of this concept has been made the centre of modern ethics. This has been done partly under the influence of former metaphysical theories of ethics, and partly as a result of the concentration on act and choice, rather than descriptive or speculative discussion, as being the essence of morality. It has been assumed that moral argument always takes the form of pointing to facts, rather than the form of analysing or explaining concepts. On the current view, freedom is conceived as freedom of overt choice, and there is a corresponding lack of interest in differences of belief. Moral language is taken as closely related to choice — that it recommends to action is its defining characteristic — and all this can then be offered as an analysis of the meaning of the word 'good'. 'This is good' equals 'choose this'. But our freedom is not just a freedom to choose and act differently, it is also a freedom to think and believe differently, to see the world differently, to see different configurations and describe them in different words. Moral differences can be differences of concept as well as differences of choice. A moral change shows in our vocabulary. How we see and describe the world is morals too — and the relation of this to our conduct may be complicated.

We were too impressed by words when we assumed that the word 'good' covered a single concept which was the centre of morality. We were not impressed enough when we neglected less general moral words such as 'true', 'brave', 'free', 'sincere', which are the bearers of very important ideas. The concept of 'goodness', for reasons which it would be interesting to investigate, is no longer a rich and problematic concept. Whereas the concept of 'truth', for instance, contains tangles and paradoxes the unravelling of which would show us really interesting features of the modern world. It is in terms of the inner complexity of such concepts that we may display really deep differences of moral vision.

It is, of course, always the philosopher's task to study the writings of philosophers of the past impartially, and compare and contrast them with ourselves. There has been of late something of a tendency to read back into the great metaphysicians our own logical formulae, and to treat them as if they were trying ineptly to do what we have done successfully. But the main task is the task on which moral philosophy is in fact engaged — the analysis of contemporary moral concepts, through moral language. I have suggested that this task has been too narrowly conceived. We have not considered the great *variety* of the concepts that make up a morality. Nor have moral philosophers made any satisfactory frontal attack on the question of how belief in the transcendent may modify the meaning of ethical statements. This question, so far as it has come up, has mainly arisen as a by-product of criticism of theological statements.

Would this sort of analysis, in its more extended form, be itself a kind of metaphysics? In a way obviously not. It does not involve the postulation of transcendent entities established by philosophical arguments; on the contrary, it is critical of all such arguments, and if it speaks of such entities they are considered as objects of faith or belief. Modern philosophy is profoundly anti-metaphysical in spirit. Its anti-metaphysical character may be summed up in the *caveat*: There may be no deep structure. This is the lesson of Wittgenstein — and one which, incidentally, has not yet been taken enough to heart by those who want to reduce morality to a single formula.

On the other hand, to analyse and describe our own morality and that of others may involve the making of models and pictures of what different kinds of men are like. Moral philosophers in the past differed concerning what they supposed themselves to be doing. Some (*e.g.* Plato) attempted to reveal a truth which was not accessible to all men. Others (*e.g.* Kant) tried to analyse the morality of any ordinary conscientious person. Philosophers who attempted the latter have usually found themselves bound to coin new concepts in making the attempt, and have not in the past been shy of doing so. And it is here that description moves imperceptibly into moralizing. An instance of a modern moral philosopher, not in our tradition, who coins new and persuasive concepts in the course of offering a description is Gabriel Marcel. Indeed all the existentialists do this. So, in a more sober way, did some of our own fairly recent philosophical ancestors — A. E. Taylor and Joseph, for instance. Even, in a way, Moore. But we have been shy of such extensive description and shy of coining concepts because we are anxious not to moralize, and because we think that ethics should study the logical structure of moral language and have the neutrality of logic. If I am right, this has merely had the result that philosophers have done their moralizing unconsciously instead of consciously.

Philosophers have usually tended to seek for universal formulae. But the linguistic method, if we take it seriously, is by its nature opposed to this search. Logic, whatever that may be determined to be, has its own universality; but when we leave the domain of the purely logical we come into the cloudy and shifting domain of the concepts which men live by — and these are subject to historical change. This is especially true of moral concepts. Here we shall have done something if we can establish with tolerable clarity what these concepts *are*. We should, I think, resist the temptation to unify the picture by trying to establish, guided by our own conception of the ethical in general, what these concepts *must be*. All that is made clear by this method is : our own conception of the ethical in general — and in the process important differences of moral concept may be blurred or neglected. Can the moral philosopher, once he stops being critical and begins to be positive, establish anything at all in the nature of a universal truth ? If by universal truth is meant something which has a sort of logical universality, then I think the answer is no. The current would-be logical analysis of moral judgments is certainly not such a truth. The difficulty is, and here we are after all not so very far from the philosophers of the past, that the subject of investigation is the nature of man — and we are studying this nature at a point of great conceptual sensibility. Man is a creature who makes pictures of himself and then comes to resemble the picture. This is the process which moral philosophy must attempt to describe and analyse.

I think it still remains for us to find a satisfactory method for the explanation of our own morality and that of others — but I think it would be a pity if, just because we realize that any picture is likely to be half a description and half a persuasion, we were to deny ourselves the freedom in the making of pictures and the coining of explanatory ideas which our predecessors have used in the past. After all, both as philosophers and as moral beings we are concerned with the same problems with which they were concerned: What is freedom? Can it be shown that men are free? What is the relation of morality to social realities? What is the relation of morality to what we believe concerning God and the hereafter? It is a merit of modern philosophers to be more conscious than their predecessors of what the philosopher's activity is. We can become more patient and historical in analysing other moralities and more daring and imaginative in exploring our own without losing the benefit of that greater consciousness.

CRITICISMS OF METAPHYSICS

METAPHYSICS has never been without its critics. Metaphysical writing, at its best at any rate, is both unique and peculiarly striking; it powerfully invites the taking of sides. There is probably no other kind of writing, at least of a sort not primarily literary, so singularly liable to seem, at some times and to some people, so immensely important, and, at other times or to other people, so entirely useless. It would be impossible to deny that respect or distaste for metaphysics is, though no doubt it should be an intellectual matter, in fact very largely a matter of temperament; and disagreements of this variety are notoriously liable to be heated and vehement, liable also to be long drawn out, inconclusive, and rather unprofitable. Not only particular theories, but metaphysics in general, have often been attacked with more fervour than understanding; and they have often been defended in a similar manner. But in this talk I shall not attempt to describe or explain either the metaphysical or the anti-metaphysical temperament; nor shall I offer a potted history of the whole highly obscure, and often confused, opposition to metaphysics. I shall concentrate instead on two kinds of criticism of metaphysics, which share at least the important virtue of being reasonably systematic and reasonably clear; these are, first, that of Logical Positivism, and second, that of Kant. I reverse the historical order for the sake of simplicity.

It is important to remember that hostility to metaphysics was not co-incidental in Logical Positivism, not a by-product of interest in other philosophical enquiries. The so-called 'elimination of metaphysics' was an explicitly proclaimed objective. And this elimination was intended to be final and complete. The suggestion was not that this theory or that was mistaken or unprofitable, but rather that *any* metaphysical theory, and indeed any metaphysical assertion, was in principle impossible, without sense or content, meaningless; and this thesis was supposed to be established by wholly rigorous proof. It was supposed not to be necessary to examine and refute in detail particular theories, one at a time; the aim was rather to show that, once an assertion or body of assertions is recognized as, or is admitted to be, metaphysical in character, then it can be dismissed without further enquiry as consisting, in Hume's phrase, of nothing but 'sophistry and illusion'.

The course of the argument could be set out in several ways. Perhaps the simplest would be the following. It would presumably be agreed that the propositions of which any metaphysical theory is composed are intended to fall within the general class of statements; they are offered for our attention as being truths. It must accordingly be fair to ask how these alleged truths are established. They might be said to be *a priori*, necessary truths, established purely by reasoning. But this, the Positivist contends, is to say that they are true in virtue of the general rules for the use of language; their necessity consists in the fact that to deny them would be to break the rules, to contradict one's self. But this in turn is to say that their necessity rests ultimately on tautology; and if so, in a sense they say nothing, their truth is purely formal and abstract. But if they are not of this character, if they are fact-stating and not purely formal, then surely some observation is required in order to determine whether what they say is in fact the case, is the case or not. But observation can only be *empirical* observation; so that the whole enquiry should be removed forthwith from the philosopher's study, and put to the test of proper experimental investigation.

Of course the Positivists assumed, rightly no doubt, that neither of the alternatives thus offered would be acceptable to the metaphysician. He would manifestly not be prepared to admit that his doctrines ought to be subjected to experimental tests, as if they were a kind of contribution to natural science; nor would he be willing to admit that they stated no facts at all, that their validity was purely formal and ultimately dependent simply upon the rules of logic and language. However, the Positivist now asserts, there is nothing else that his doctrines can be — unless indeed their claim to be truths is abandoned, and they are offered merely as a kind of poetry or incantatory rhetoric. The metaphysician may indeed try to claim that not all facts are empirical facts, and hence that not all statements of fact are capable of confirmation or falsification by observation; but this is dismissed as hollow pretension. For if we do not know what sort of observations or experiences would confirm or falsify a statement, we do not know what it means; and if we are told that *no* observations or experiences would confirm or falsify it, this can only amount to the admission that it has no meaning. If it means anything it must in principle at least be testable. And here is the Positivist's central contention. To verify or falsify a statement of fact, he says, is to discover, of course by observation, whether or not that situation obtains which it asserts to obtain; to say of any alleged statement that it cannot in principle thus be verified or falsified must amount to saying that there is *no* situation which it asserts to obtain; and this in turn amounts to saying that it has no meaning. It thus appears that the metaphysician, if he is to save his doctrines, must present them *either* as abstract theories, quite devoid of factual content, like pure mathematics, *or* as bodies of experimentally testable statements of fact. But he could not take either of these courses while continuing to be a metaphysician; so it remains only that he must cease to be so. What he thought to be his serious subject has simply dissolved into non-significance. The idea that there is a class of metaphysical truths, distinct both from truths of common experience or natural science and from formal tautologies without factual content, has turned out, it appears, to be pure illusion; once we see what it is for any statement to have meaning, we see that in principle there cannot be metaphysical statements. To say that an alleged assertion is metaphysical amounts to saying that it is bogus, a pseudo-assertion at best, sheer rigmarole at worst.

I shall attempt to assess the real weight of this attack a little later. At the moment I would like to emphasize this one point. The attack on metaphysics thus delivered is, in a certain sense, indirect. It consists, not primarily in the critical scrutiny of metaphysical doctrines, but in a classification of types of significant utterances, leading to the conclusion that none of the types so classified is metaphysical. Thus metaphysics is indeed eliminated, rather than destroyed; it is not exploded, but extruded; it is simply cast out from the field of significant discourse. Hence the positivistic attack rests crucially on the assumption that its classification of types of significant discourse is complete; for if it were not, to extrude metaphysics from this classification would not amount to a demonstration of its non-significance.

The position of Kant in the history of anti-metaphysics is more complicated, in proportion as his criticism was more subtle, richer and more sympathetic. At two important points his approach was a better one than was the rather high-handed onslaught of Logical Positivism. First, the Positivistic attack is liable to leave one with the impression that metaphysics has merely been defined out of existence. Metaphysics appears to be characterized almost solely in such a way as to facilitate its eventual destruction. Kant by contrast attempted a serious and not unsympathetic diagnosis of the actual character of metaphysical assertions. Second, the recent Positivistic attack has the defect of making it seem almost incredible that men, usually of uncommon ability, should have devoted themselves with such industry and persistence to propounding doctrines which were all, the critics allege, simply non-significant. Kant by contrast rightly thought it essential to explain why the inclination to metaphysical theorizing should be, as it manifestly has been, so very strong, and so strong particularly in men of high intelligence. His criticism does not make metaphysics look merely absurd, or appear merely as an inexplicable divagation from sense.

As we saw, the Positivistic elimination of metaphysics rested essentially on the claim that any significant proposition, if it is not a mere formal tautology without factual content, must be in principle capable of being confirmed or falsified by observation; if it says anything, experience alone can show whether what it says is the case or not. Now Kant was familiar with this idea, which had in effect been put forward by his predecessor Hume; he thought it an idea of the greatest importance, but nevertheless he could not accept it. For he thought that there are two sorts of things we can say about human experience. First, we can say what particular features it actually has; and here he agreed that we must employ observation and experiment to discover whether in fact it has these features or not. But second, we can also say, according to Kant, what very general features human experience *must* have, if there is to be such a thing as human experience at all; we can state, as he puts it, the conditions of the *possibility* of experience; and here, he concluded, there is no place for seeking confirmation *by* experience. For of course, if a statement states a condition of the possibility of experience, it is impossible that experience should show it to be false, and hence unnecessary to consult experience to establish its truth. However, a statement of this kind, according to Kant, is not metaphysical in any disreputable sense; for it is, he thinks, capable of the most rigorous proof, and in any case still says something about our experience, even though experience can neither falsify nor confirm it. Such a statement would be, in Kant's technical language, synthetic and *a priori* at the same time, fact-stating but also necessarily true.

From this point Kant proceeds to the examination of a group of ideas of a very different sort. Let us take some examples. We are inclined, he says, to think of the Universe, its nature and its history as being in principle completely knowable. We realize, of course, that our actual experience and knowledge of it are inevitably partial and limited; no doubt we do not think that we ourselves can sensibly aspire to know everything about everything. But we still do, he says, have the idea that what we do know is a fragment of some ideal whole, that what we experience is a part of some *totality* of things and events. Rather similarly we have, he says, the ideal of some final and absolute explanation. Here, too, we are aware that our own explanations of events are given merely in terms of further events, which themselves stand in need of yet further explanation; but as we extend our always limited power to explain, we think of ourselves as making some approach to a

goal, getting nearer to the standpoint, which doubtless in fact we shall never reach, from which everything could be wholly explained without any re-
mainder. The central concept here is that of
completeness; our powers and our experience are
always limited, but as we seek to extend our knowledge and our understanding, we are impelled to
think of ourselves as getting fractionally closer to
the ideal goal of complete knowledge, and complete
understanding, of the sum of things.

Now Kant sees the metaphysician as a thinker
obsessed by this ideal of completeness. He seeks the
explanation not of this or that, but of everything;
he seeks to know the nature, not of some things, but
of all things; he is interested, not in particular times
or places, but in the whole of Space and of Time.
He may be interested, as Leibniz was, in the ultimate
elements of which everything consists, and the
ultimate reason for which anything occurs. He may
be a theologian, finding in God's will the first cause
and ultimate explanation of the whole Creation.
He may be a deist, as (roughly) Spinoza was, conceiving the totality of things as a coherent system
called indifferently God or Nature. But in any case
he will be concerned, in one way or another, with
the *ultimate* nature of the *whole* of Reality, with the
first cause, the *final* explanation, the *complete* account.

Suppose then (to take a somewhat over-simple
example) that a particular metaphysician conceives
of the Universe as a totality, finite in space and time,
of things and events, and maintains that the ultimate
explanation of its existence and character must lie
outside it, in the will and purposes of a single Supreme

Being. What would Kant's comment be upon such a doctrine? He would regard it as an amalgam of complete mistakes and illusions. Take first the question of finiteness in space and time. What possible observations, Kant would ask, could entitle us to conclude that the Universe either is or is not finite? How could we know, does it even make sense to say, either that we had reached, observed and established its boundaries, or that we had tried to do so and failed? And if the metaphysician claims to produce an *a priori* proof that the Universe must be finite, Kant claims that he could always produce another proof, no better and no worse, to show that it could not possibly be finite. And what do we know of a Supreme Being? To say that such a being must lie outside the scope of our always limited experience is to admit that in fact we can know nothing about it, and are merely spinning words when we purport to state its character and purposes. Indeed, Kant would say that the characteristic aim of any metaphysician, the aim of acquiring knowledge not of the always limited and conditioned objects of actual experience but of that totality of things which transcends all limits and all experience, is itself enough to make it quite clear that the aims of metaphysics cannot be achieved. We are human beings; our knowledge and understanding are necessarily confined to the field of possible human experience; if we seek to transcend this limitation we may indeed continue to talk, but we necessarily cease to understand what we are saying. Outside these limits we can neither affirm nor deny. Let me quote two passages to show Kant's position. 'There is', he says, 'no polemic in the field of pure reason [*i.e.* in metaphysics]. Both parties beat the air, and wrestle with their own shadows, since they go beyond the limits of nature, where there is nothing that they can seize and hold with their dogmatic grasp. Fight as they may, the shadows which they cleave asunder grow together again forthwith, like the heroes in Valhalla, to disport themselves anew in the bloodless contests.' And a little earlier he says, 'Whenever I hear that a writer of real ability has demonstrated away the freedom of the human will, the hope of a future life, and the existence of God, I am eager to read the book, for I expect him by his talents to increase my insight into these matters. Already, before having opened it, I am perfectly certain that he has not justified any one of his specific claims; not because I believe that I am in possession of conclusive proofs of these important propositions, but because . . . [I am] . . . completely convinced that, as reason is incompetent to arrive at affirmative assertions in this field, it is equally unable . . . to establish any negative conclusion in regard to these questions. . . . [They are] outside the field of possible experience, and therefore beyond the limits of all human insight.' He adds that the orthodox metaphysician's defence, say, of the existence of God, he would not bother to read at all; for the false arguments he would have to use would not even be new. Controversy between metaphysical schools, he says, is 'indeed toilsome to the combatants, but for us can be entertaining; and its outcome — certain to be quite bloodless — must be of advantage as contributing to our theoretical insight'. Quite vain though these controversies are, they sharpen our wits.

This insistence that our knowledge and understanding are confined to the field of possible experience, and that the metaphysical ambition to transcend this leads only to word-spinning and fighting with shadows, no doubt inclines us to expect that Kant will condemn metaphysics as foolish and useless, perhaps meaningless, as the Positivists did. On the contrary. He not only regards metaphysics with respect and affection; he regards it as an almost *unavoidable* temptation and challenge to the human intellect. 'Human reason', he writes, 'can never dispense with such a science. . . . However cold or contemptuously critical may be the attitude of those who judge a science not by its nature but by its accidental effects, we shall always return to metaphysics as to a beloved one with whom we have had a quarrel. For here we are concerned with essential ends.' Although we may be, as he says, perfectly certain that we shall thus achieve no extension of our knowledge, the attempt will never be given up. 'For here we have to do with a *natural* and inevitable *illusion* . . . — not one in which a bungler might entangle himself through lack of knowledge, or one which some sophist has artificially invented to confuse thinking people, but one inseparable from human reason.'

In Kant's opinion there are two main reasons why we must not, and indeed cannot, abandon metaphysics completely. The first is theoretical, the second practical. In the first place, he thinks that as we attempt systematically to extend our knowledge and understanding of the world, we cannot help having the idea that our investigations are in principle completable, that there is some totality of things and some final explanation, even if in our sober moments we do not hope to reach any absolutely final conclusion. If we did not have, and were not guided by, this idea, Kant thinks that we could no longer persist in our efforts; it is practically essential to our persisting in the task that we should *think* of it *as* in principle completable, even if we know that in reality this ideal is an empty one. And consequently there must be a constant temptation, particularly for the most persistent and ambitious investigators, to think of this ideal not merely as an incentive and a guide, but as a truth. What we cannot help thinking, we will always be tempted to suppose that we could know; and in this supposition is the germ of metaphysics.

In the second place, Kant held that our moral experience made it imperative to think of the world as the creation of an omnipotent and omniscient being, of people as free and immortal spirits, of this life as the prelude to an endless life after death, of the course of world history as somehow purposive and planned. We cannot know, he insists, that any of this is true; but equally we cannot help thinking of the world in this way. Indeed, so important did he consider it to be that we should think in this way, that he holds that his critical exposure of metaphysical false claims really renders an important service to the theologian and the metaphysical moralist. It would, he thinks, be absolutely disastrous if it could be shown that there is no God, no immortality, no freedom of will, no purpose in the course of history; but his demonstration of the impossibility of knowing anything at all about these matters of course ensures that denials are just as baseless as affirmations; atheism is in no better case than theology itself. We may be quite sure, then, that when we think of the world and of ourselves as the creation of an all-powerful and benevolent God it can never be shown that we are mistaken. We must think in this way, and we may be sure that we always can. But equally we shall be constantly tempted into supposing that what we thus think we could also know; and here again is the germ from which metaphysics springs. The metaphysical enterprise, though strictly it is purely illusory, is thus in two ways natural to human reason; there will always be thinkers disposed to embark upon it; and in Kant's view, though strictly there is nothing to hope for from their labours, they still deserve the respect and attention of reasonable men. They are likely, in an indirect and peculiar way, to be doing good.

Let me now try to assess the true force of these two criticisms of metaphysics. The Positivistic attack, although I believe its sharp impact has been on the whole advantageous, seems to me to be philosophically unsatisfying — not so much because it gets to a mistaken conclusion, as because it seems to get to this conclusion too quickly. Its classification of the types of significant discourse is in any case vulnerable in countless points of detail; but more importantly, if metaphysics is to be eliminated, it is surely necessary to determine what its aims and its character are, and to show that just these aims are vain and this character vicious. Here Logical Positivism leaves one dissatisfied. It is indeed made clear enough that a metaphysical theory has not the kind of claim to acceptance which a scientific theory has; that it is neither exposed to falsification, nor capable of support, in the way in which scientific theories are. Perhaps more importantly, I think it is also made clear that scientific theories themselves do not require the support of metaphysical doctrines, and are not to be attacked on metaphysical grounds; and historically this defence of the autonomy of the sciences was an important part of the Positivist programme. But neither of these points, important though they are, supplies the lack of any serious attempt to decide what a metaphysical theory positively is. These critics seem to have cast at metaphysics too hasty and too unsympathetic a glance; their hope was to explode the whole of metaphysical literature without putting themselves or us to the painful necessity of reading it. Whatever it is, they wished to say, it can't be any use. But inevitably those who were unsympathetic to this attack felt that metaphysics was being dismissed without being understood; and the verdict of 'Meaningless' was too abusive to suggest or encourage a fair trial of the case. It is, by contrast, as I mentioned before, an important merit of Kant that he did try to understand what metaphysics is, and did not so explain its defects as to make it incredible that intelligent men should ever have been metaphysicians. He did go through many metaphysical arguments in detail, and sought with enormous industry and penetration to locate at each stage the particular error.

He achieved, I think, also an important general insight. The Positivist shows us *that* metaphysical doctrines are not susceptible of ordinary confirmation and falsification ; Kant suggests an answer to the question *why* not. To put it roughly, the metaphysician takes some concept which is ordinarily applied, rightly or wrongly, within a particular field, and proceeds to apply it to the whole of that field ; but since the contrast between right and wrong application lies *within* this field, its application to the *whole* field abolishes the possibility of contrast. For example : in the field of human affairs some things are done of set purpose and some are not ; the assertion that a particular thing was done of set purpose may be, and may be shown to be, either true or false. But if the metaphysical assertion is made that *everything* occurs in pursuance of the purposes of God, this implies that there neither are nor could be any events occurring not in pursuance of those purposes. But if so, in principle nothing that occurred could count against the assertion, and nothing in particular that occurs counts in its favour. Now hence it disconcertingly appears that it makes no difference whether we make the assertion or deny it ; as Kant says, there can be 'no polemic in the field of pure reason', for there is no way of settling our apparent disagreements. But on Kant's view this sort of lapse into vacuousness is neither inexplicable, nor wholly useless. It is not useless, he thinks, for though we can neither affirm nor deny that the world *is in fact* controlled by the purposes of God, we both can and should try to *think* of it *as* thus controlled; and it is not inexplicable, in that the metaphysical assertion is only the last and fatally over-ambitious application of a concept which, up to that point, we quite properly employ.

Are we then to conclude that Kant's analysis of the powers, and limitations, and characteristic misuses of human reason was in fact as exhaustive and final as he, with pardonable pride, claimed that it was? Did he succeed in finally 'placing' metaphysics, and in drawing its sting so far as that can be done? I think that we cannot concede to him quite so much as this. The trouble is that metaphysics is more various and more Hydra-headed even than he was ready to recognize. Indeed, as was said in the opening discussion of this series, there is in Kant's own work a prominent strain which itself can well be called metaphysical. And this shows itself in two ways. In the first place, in spite of his repeated insistence that our understanding is confined within the field of possible experience, and that the metaphysical sin consists essentially in the attempt to transcend this limitation, he himself did not hesitate to contrast the world of human experience, as 'appearance', with a real world of 'things in themselves' in principle unexperienceable. Curiously, he felt no incompatibility between a firm conviction of the *existence* of this 'real' world and the admission that nothing whatever could be known about it. But in the second place, and this perhaps is a more central point, his own belief was that we could discover, once and for all, the essential, absolutely fundamental features of any possible human experience; although he did not believe that it was possible, so to speak, to step outside experience, he did believe that it was possible to arrive at a completely general and final characterization of it from within. He had, as at the start of this series the metaphysician was said characteristically to have, an interest in 'the whole map', in the fundamental concepts which we employ, not in this or that particular context, but everywhere. But if Kant can draw out this whole map in one way, why should not a rival theorist re-draw it in another way? There can here be no question of saying that only some particular fundamental concepts will be found applicable to human experience; for, as Kant himself insisted, the character of human experience is partly determined by the concepts which human beings employ. To attempt, as Kant did, a kind of basic conceptual classification seems to leave open to the metaphysician the project of conceptual revision. If this is impossible Kant does not tell us why; and could it be shown to be impossible without calling in question the legitimacy of his own procedure? This question could be put in a more technical form, by asking how far Kant could really maintain the distinction between his own supposedly demonstrable 'metaphysic of nature', and the illusory, 'dialectical' metaphysic which he condemns.

Thus, even Kant's criticism of metaphysics, most powerful and penetrating though it was, cannot be held to have closed the question. It is doubtless possible to describe in general terms certain intellectual enterprises, reasonably to be called metaphysical, which if undertaken one could show were in principle illusory and insubstantial. But in particular cases there is no substitute for attempting to discern the aims of a particular writer, and attempting to assess the merits of his particular arguments. And this task is always liable to be complicated by the fact that philosophers, perhaps the best of them above all, are apt to be most unreliable judges of the nature of their own doctrines and intentions. They mislead us; and of course we also mislead ourselves; even those who are convinced that metaphysics is a trap to be avoided are liable to walk into the trap without realizing where they are going. By this fact, however, Kant at least would not have been surprised. It is only intermittently, he would have said, that we can emancipate ourselves from the frailties of human reason.

FINAL DISCUSSION

ANTHONY QUINTON. One thing that makes our task of winding up these essays easier is the considerable measure of agreement among our predecessors in the series as to what metaphysics is. A widely accepted point of view on this issue has been indicated by their recurrent references to conceptual revision. It has been held that the real point of constructing a metaphysical system is the recommendation of a conceptual framework, a set of concepts, that is, that can be applied to the whole of our experience and will do full justice to it. As it is we describe and explain what happens in the world with a number of partly independent, partly overlapping systems of concepts — physical, biological, psychological. But these partial systems we recognize to be selective and their application to the same subject-matter sometimes leads to conflict. A metaphysical system resolves these conflicts by picking out one partial system of concepts and counting it as the finally adequate instrument for description and explanation, while all other partial systems are relegated to the status of useful but not wholly trustworthy practical devices. We shall have to consider later the objections that have been raised to the way in which these conceptual revisions have been argued for. But it must be admitted that they have often been useful. The metaphysical view of nature put forward by Descartes — that the physical world is a system of extended material bodies, mechanically interacting and endowed only with measurable qualities — at once stimulated and established the terms of reference of seventeenth-century physics. And it might be argued that the metaphysics of Hegel had a comparable influence on historical studies in the nineteenth century. So, to interpret metaphysics as the proposal of unitary conceptual schemes is not to treat it as an unimportant or wholly mistaken undertaking.

MARY WARNOCK. The other aspect of metaphysics that was stressed was its comprehensiveness. Several of the speakers discussed the claims of metaphysical systems to give us a total and complete kind of knowledge; that is, to provide a total explanation of everything. I should think it would not be going too far to say that some such claim is essential to a metaphysical system. They all in some way attempt to get beyond the limits of ordinary, hypothetical and incomplete human knowledge to something absolutely satisfactory and complete.

A. Q. This view that metaphysics tries to state what would be complete knowledge or a complete explanation of the universe may be misleading. For the metaphysician does not set out to compile an encyclopaedia by his characteristically demonstrative method. Admittedly Hegel, and possibly Leibniz to some extent, believed in the encyclopaedic potentialities of metaphysical argument, but this belief is not widespread or characteristic of metaphysicians. They tell us, rather, what *kind* of universe we inhabit. With this reservation in mind the connection between the two interpretations becomes clearer. For to describe the *structure* of the universe, to say what *kind* of thing it is as a whole — the rational project of an intelligent being, for example, or a machine — is to imply what sort of conceptual system is appropriate for describing it.

GILBERT RYLE. This is all very well. But a philosopher would not usually rank as a metaphysician just for his contributions to the task of conceptual revision ; and he might very well rank as a metaphysician even though the navigators of the sciences got no advice from him in setting their theoretical courses. What is commonly expected of a metaphysician is that he should assert the existence or occurrence of things unseen and give for these assertions purely philosophical or conceptual reasons. If he is not an ontologist he is not a metaphysician.

More specifically, the metaphysician is widely expected to argue for existence-conclusions which either belong to theology or are at least theologically interesting. Sometimes these conclusions are theologically interesting because, like Materialism, Deism and Pantheism, they are theologically shocking. After all, 'theology' was the word that Aristotle himself used for the constructive core of what was posthumously entitled his 'Metaphysics'. When people nowadays lament the moribund condition of metaphysics, it is constructive philosophical theology or near-theology that they are apt to miss.

Naturally, theological philosophers could, on the side, be concept-revisers and navigation-consultants. Or their theological ideas could be the source and the control of their ideas in these other domains. Still, it is not for these mundane but for those supramundane ideas that they are celebrated or castigated as metaphysicians.

The fact that our forerunners in this series were almost silent about this fairly traditional connotation of the label 'metaphysician' is symptomatic of our remoteness from the inter-theological and anti-theological zeals of only two or three generations ago. We hardly notice the noteworthy fact that our tributes to former metaphysicians are purely secular tributes. Perhaps there are no other tributes to pay, but the shades of our grandfathers must be surprised to find us already taking this for granted.

M. W. I agree that the connection with theology has been a very important feature of metaphysics; but I don't think it is actually essential to it. The desire to adopt some metaphysical system often seems to arise out of a very general desire to consider human beings and human life in some wider context — in fact a context which is to include everything. Metaphysicians themselves seem to have aimed at this, and people who are not philosophers at all expect metaphysicians to provide them with some such wider framework in which to see themselves.

A. Q. You mean people want to see how human beings fit in with whatever else the universe may contain?

M. W. Yes, and this can of course lead them to a religious system of some kind, in which, for instance, human life is seen as fulfilling some divine purpose. But it need not lead them in this direction.

Materialism is a metaphysical system as well and affords a setting in which to place human beings so that they may be seen as they really are and may take on their proper proportion in relation to the rest of the universe. I think metaphysics, in this ontological aspect, has had a close connection with science as well as with religion — often, of course, to the deliberate exclusion of religion.

G. R. Hobbes would be a good example of a metaphysician of this other, scientific, kind. In maintaining that whatever is not matter forms no part of the universe he was obviously deeply influenced by seventeenth-century physical science.

A. Q. I quite agree that to say that metaphysicians propose conceptual revisions is rather to interpret their activities than to give a faithful account of what they thought they were doing. And I agree that what they intended to provide was an ontology, a general picture of the world. But it does not follow from this that they would reject the view that they were proposing conceptual revisions. For they would maintain that if an ontology, an account of the actual structure of the universe, could be demonstratively established important consequences would ensue on the conceptual level. If, for example, a materialist ontology, to the effect that the universe is really a system of material bodies influencing each other by impact, were true then it would follow that a certain conceptual system, that embodied in the language of classical mechanics, was correct and that all others, however handy for immediate practical purposes, were ultimately inadequate and misleading. The proposal of the conceptual system, then, would be justified as the *correct* proposal by the truth of the ontology.

G. R. Then surely the metaphysician would reject the interpretation of his activities as the proposal of a conceptual revision, since such an interpretation, while accepting a derivative part of his undertaking, neglects what is to him its primary and fundamental feature.

A. Q. He would reject the view that metaphysics was *merely* such a proposal since it ignores his claim about the correctness of the revisions which his ontology entails. The fact is that many, perhaps most, philosophers are now convinced that no ontological thesis can be demonstratively proved, while at the same time they are prepared to agree that the work of metaphysicians has been influential on our inherited ways of thinking. The interpretation we are considering is attractive because it explains how this influence can have been exerted despite the invalidity of its ontological foundations.

M. W. So now the question arises as to how conceptual revisions are to be justified, always supposing they can be justified at all.

A. Q. Assuming for the moment that revisions cannot be based on demonstrated ontologies, there would seem to be three possible positions one could hold. First, a conservative, even quietist, line could be taken to the effect that our existing conceptual apparatus is perfectly all right as it is and that the conflicts and perplexities that confront us from time to time arise from our incompetent handling of it. On this view the task of philosophy is the local and piecemeal clarification of our existing conceptual equipment and not its reform or replacement as a whole. This view is a sort of Burkean caricature of the later doctrines of Wittgenstein.

M. W. Surely Wittgenstein would not have denied that our conceptual apparatus could be changed. Look at what he says about language games.

A. Q. He did not deny that it could be changed; but he did not think that it was necessary to revise it or that it was the business of philosophers to carry out the revision. Another point of view, at the opposite extreme, is the kind of conceptual libertarianism which Carnap seems sometimes to support. This holds that there is nothing to prevent your choosing any consistent conceptual scheme you like, except perhaps its complexity or unfamiliarity. Finally, and in my opinion more reasonably, it could be held that conceptual systems, like the scientific theories which we use them to formulate, are subject to the pragmatic test of trial and error. The system of mechanical concepts that Descartes proposed for seventeenth-century physics — mass, velocity, acceleration and so forth — has been applied with triumphant success. On the other hand what system of concepts should be applied in the large-scale empirical study of human behaviour is still an open question. Theoretical economics, for example, has in recent years been disembarrassing itself of the concepts of utilitarian psychology in whose terms its foundations have been traditionally expressed.

G. R. Let us turn to the question whether the attempt to prove ontological theses demonstratively is mistaken. Hume and Kant exposed the fallaciousness of all arguments from purely conceptual considerations to positive existence-conclusions and none of our present team has, I gather, any inclination to rehabilitate them. Ontologizing is out. The factual parts of cosmological and theological doctrines must stand, if at all, on floors of which philosophy is not the landlord.

There is no need to pull long faces over these negations. Astronomers, in their task of determining the paths of the planets, have gained and not lost by switching from the methods of Aristotle to those of Kepler, from would-be *a priori* arguments to the evidence of the telescope. Nor, on the other hand, is it any slur upon philosophical reasonings that they are incompetent to establish particular matters of planetary fact. Theirs is quite a different sort of business and one which is not impeded but assisted by the recognition of its differences.

It may be protested: 'Oh, but while astronomy certainly is infinitely better off with empirical evidence than with *a priori* considerations for its basis, this is not true of theology. The factual conclusions of astronomy are inferences to things visible from the evidence of things seen. But the factual conclusions of theology, being inferences to things invisible, must take their start from non-observational premisses. Who can supply these premisses, if not the metaphysician?' It is easy to see through this protest. It is like the protest of the traveller who, when refused petrol by the railway-station, insisted that the sweetshop must be able to supply him, since he could not drive home otherwise.

The reason why ontology is out is quite simple. Any assertion of the existence of something, like any assertion of the occurrence of something, can be denied without logical absurdity. So the reasons for assertions of existence or occurrence can never be purely conceptual considerations. We may indeed and often do have the best possible reasons for concluding to the existence or occurrence of something; but these reasons must themselves embody factual evidence, evidence got by experimental as distinct from merely conceptual investigations. When we want to know what there actually is or what has actually gone on in the universe, we have to quarry in the appropriate parts of the universe itself. Quarrying cannot be replaced by architect's desk-work, any more than eating can be replaced by digesting. Still less can quarrying for evidence be replaced by philosophizing. For philosophizing is the second-order business of tracing the structural stresses that develop between the technical theories or the untechnical schemes of ideas of which our factual findings are the stones.

A. Q. Certainly there are a number of general objections that can be raised to the project of ontological demonstration. No truths about what exists can be proved to be logically necessary; or, to put much the same point in verificationist terms, there can be no substantially informative statements about the world which are immune from refutation by the course of our experience. Again, concepts that we can apply *within* the world cannot necessarily or even normally be applied intelligibly to the world as a whole. But these considerations are too general to carry conviction. They need the support of critical examination of concrete instances of metaphysical demonstration.

Let me take a simple and famous example — the ontological proof of God's existence. This starts from the reasonable enough definition of God as the most perfect being, as that nothing more perfect than which can be conceived. Now consider two things identical in every respect except that one exists and the other does not. Clearly the one that exists is the more perfect. Suppose that God does not exist. Then something more perfect than he can be conceived, namely something identical with him in every respect but which also exists. So the God we have supposed is, by definition, not God. To suppose that God does not exist entails a contradiction and, therefore, God must necessarily exist. Now this argument, as many theologians would agree, depends on the mistaken presumption that existence is a property. As Hume put it, there is no difference between conceiving something and conceiving that it exists: to conceive a thing *is* to conceive it as existing. Existence is a formal concept; this argument treats it as if it were a non-formal one like persistence or resistance.

M. W. Locke's proof that every event has a cause is equally manageable. Suppose something took place without a cause. Then we could say it was caused by nothing. But it is impossible for nothing to be the cause of something. So everything must be caused by something, every event has a cause. Here again the argument hinges on a play with a formal concept. The crucial stage in the argument — it is impossible for nothing to be the cause of something — can be interpreted in two ways. On one interpretation it simply begs the question at issue by asserting that it is impossible for a thing to have no cause. But Locke seems to interpret it in another way, as stating, roughly, that Nothing is far too feeble and evanescent an affair to be capable of exerting a causal influence. This is to understand the sentence 'nothing caused this' as meaning 'the entity Nothing-with-a-capital-N brought this about'; a senseless but beguiling travesty of 'this has no cause'.

A. Q. Of course not all metaphysical demonstrations are as easy to criticize as these, and I would not maintain that they all rested quite so squarely on the misuse of formal concepts like Existence and Nothing. But for all their simplicity these examples are representative and there is a positive reward — in the increased understanding we achieve of formal concepts — to be acquired from the piecemeal criticism of metaphysical arguments as well as the negative reward of exposing the deficiencies of demonstrative ontology.

M. W. One point which strikes me is that there is a danger in talking about 'metaphysical arguments' or 'metaphysical demonstrations' or 'metaphysical statements' as if they formed some clearly defined and easily recognizable class. The suggestion may seem to be that, once having identified such arguments or statements we can see that they have some features in common and can proceed to refute them or criticize them wholesale. But in fact I don't think it is possible to treat them in this way. There are no criteria by which one may test a given statement to see whether it is metaphysical or not. Absolutely any statement could be metaphysical — and any argument could, equally, be a metaphysical argument. The test is what the argument is being used for or what the statement means in its context. And if we can't apply any ready-made test to statements to separate the metaphysical from the non-metaphysical, it follows that we shall have to consider every statement on its merits. There will be no ready-made refutations either. We can't try to detach statements from their contexts and show that they either are or aren't metaphysical. And I think it follows from this that, if metaphysics is to be criticized, it should be criticized by something like Kant's methods rather than the methods of the logical positivists. Kant did go through metaphysical arguments one by one — at least he went through several. He didn't rule them all out without looking at them.

A. Q. I think you are letting your doubts about the preciseness of the word 'metaphysical' carry you too far. Certainly some people nowadays do tend to use the word of any philosophical remark of which they disapprove, or, a little less generally, of any paradoxical, counter-intuitive philosophical thesis. But this is a very familiar sort of linguistic bad habit; consider the employment in heated political discussions of such labels of insult as 'communist' and 'fascist'. I would agree that there is no complete criterion for a statement's being metaphysical, but this does not mean that any statement may be metaphysical, for we can surely lay down the negative requirement that no statement can be metaphysical unless it is at once substantial, not a definitional truism, and highly general. But a statement may have these features and yet not be metaphysical. What we must also look to are the reasons for which it is made. As was pointed out in an earlier essay it would not be metaphysical to say that all human actions are selfish, if one were to base the assertion on an embittering experience of life, rather than on a demonstrative argument. But that a general and substantial statement is demonstrable (or thought to be so) is surely both enough and necessary to show that it is metaphysical. It is worth emphasizing that a metaphysical statement need not be paradoxical, (I am thinking here of metaphysical demonstrations that survival of death is impossible), and a para-doxical statement need not be metaphysical, (consider the selfishness example). It was my belief that their demonstrability, real or supposed, is essential to metaphysical statements that led me to argue earlier that there was no effective substitute in the criticism of metaphysics for the examination on their merits of actual metaphysical demonstrations.

G. R. Let us, at this point, take a rest from talking about metaphysicians as if we were their examiners and they were our examinees. Let us reverse the rôles and, forgetting the good and the bad marks that we have been giving to them, con-sider instead whether we deserve the bad marks, that they, from their Olympian studio, have been giving to philosophers of our half-century. I say 'of our half-century' since people quite often lament or boast that post-Victorian philosophy has on the whole departed from its traditional ways and now speaks in an accent distressingly or encouragingly unlike that of earlier times. I agree that there has been a big change in direction and accent, though I also think that the history of philosophy records a fair number of equally big changes of direction and accent. Like the growing hermit-crab, human thought has, every now and then, to get out of its old shell and migrate into a new shell. Well then, what can we hear our metaphysical forefathers saying about us from their timeless studio? First of all, they do not speak entirely with one voice. They all mark us down for things that we do and neglect, but not all for the same things. There are Aristotle and Leibniz audibly dissenting from the strictures passed by Plotinus and Hegel upon the huge developments in our Formal Logic; and there is Kant being markedly silent while Plato reproaches us for being so much occupied with the principles and categories of the natural sciences, and the humane studies. Bradley seems equally restive when Hume applauds and when Aquinas deplores our neglect of rational theology. However, there are some things for which the majority of them seem to be agreed in scolding us. They scold us, first of all, for our sedulous refusal to talk about the cosmos. Even though, for argument's sake, they concede our excuse that matters of fact, including matters of cosmic fact, cannot be established by *a priori* reasoning, they still grumble at us for shirking altogether central issues which they, if perhaps with the wrong tools, did seriously tackle. Philosophy need not be departmentalized just because it no longer dreams of being the science of the supra-mundane. A surveyor need not be an explorer, but he can still try to piece together his local charts into a complete globe.

To this charge we had better plead guilty, though not, I suggest, with grave dejection. The time is not yet ripe for new global syntheses. For forty years the canons and apparatus of philosophical reasoning have been undergoing a continuous transformation, the culmination of which is still in the future. In the meantime we do well to educate ourselves by tactical, rather than strategic enterprises, fortifying ourselves with the thought that most of the Olympians educated themselves in the very same way.

A second unanimous grumble is that, even inside our constricted horizon, we are diligent about trivialities and neglectful of things that matter. This general grumble is unanimous because everyone, Olympian or not, tends to regard as trivial those of his colleagues' interests which he does not share, and no-one, Olympian or otherwise, can tell in advance whether his own darling line of enquiry may not end in a blind alley. It is when this grumble becomes specific that the shoe begins to pinch. There is Plato, with many supporting voices, asking why we have so little to say about the immortality of the soul; and there is Rousseau complaining that we no longer debate the source of the authority of the state. Herbert Spencer misses discussions of the bearings of evolutionary theory on the nature of man and human society, while Hobbes thinks that it is the bearings of atomic theory that are being unwarrantably neglected. So let us draw up a short list of some of our imputed sins of omission — though I hasten to say that I myself do not propose to fudge interests, simply because Olympians scold me for not having them.

A. Q. There is one line of objection which I do not think that Ryle's Olympians would advance but which is advanced with wearisome insistence on their behalf by contemporary critics of philosophy. I mean by this the view that in our obsession with Alexandrian trivialities we ignore those problems of life which are the true and traditional province of the philosopher. Instead of the clarification and understanding we offer, they call for moralizing and guidance. This is a pretty well-worn subject and diminishing returns have set in to argument about it. But where argument seems unavailing perhaps the authority of a great philosopher will be more effective. Listen to this:

'How do I get to know in particular what is right and wrong? . . . Here again we find a strangely erroneous preconception. It is thought that moral philosophy has to accomplish this task for us; and the conclusion lies near at hand that any system which will not do this is worthless. Well, we first remark and with some confidence, that there cannot be a moral philosophy which will tell us what in particular we are to do, and also that it is not the business of philosophy to do so. All philosophy has to do is to 'understand what is', and moral philosophy has to understand morals which exist, not to make them or give directions for making them. Such a notion is simply ludicrous. Philosophy in general has not to anticipate the discoveries of the particular sciences nor the evolution of history . . .

and ethics has not to make the world moral, but to reduce to theory the morality current in the world. If we want it to do anything more so much the worse for us. . . . Who would go to a learned theologian, as such, in a practical religious difficulty; to a system of aesthetic for suggestions on the handling of an artistic theme; to a physiologist, as such, for a diagnosis and prescription; to a political philosopher in practical politics; or to a psychologist in an intrigue of any kind? All these persons no doubt *might* be the best to go to, but that would not be because they were the best theorists, but because they were more.'

Well, that categorical defence of the present-day philosopher's practice comes, surprisingly enough, from F. H. Bradley, the most uncompromising of British metaphysicians.

M. W. Still, I think we should return to Ryle's point and see whether we are in fact paying enough attention to the important questions metaphysicians have asked. Perhaps we should ask ourselves whether it is true that philosophy has abandoned its proper, important and interesting province and given itself up, as the familiar cry would have it, to frivolities.

A. Q. There was an extreme example of this line of attack in a recent *Times Literary Supplement* leading article which said: 'Philosophy is at a lower ebb than it has been since the last Schoolmen argued in their attics. The successors of Bosanquet and Bradley, of McTaggart and Moore, quibble about niggling points of logic having as much relevance to reality as they have interest for the general public.'

M. W. That's just the sort of thing. I don't for a moment want to suggest that this extreme view is justified ; it is clearly an exaggeration, but an exaggeration of something perhaps often felt. The question is ought we to try to direct philosophy back to those questions with which characteristically metaphysical philosophers were chiefly concerned ? Well, there are two points to make about this. First, I don't think it is at all clear that all the questions raised by metaphysical philosophers have in fact been neglected in recent years ; and secondly, the criticisms of metaphysics which have been put forward in earlier essays cannot be disregarded. It is impossible to go on as if they had never been made. And so whatever questions should or should not be asked by philosophers, they will not be able to set about answering them in the characteristically metaphysical ways. It may be true that our interests are too narrow at the moment, but to broaden our horizons would not in fact be the same thing as to return to metaphysical system-making.

G. R. Well, let's look at a few of the things that matter which we can be accused of neglecting. In our half-century philosophy and theology have hardly been on speaking terms. Out of all the hundreds of philosophical meetings that I have attended and out of all the hundreds of articles that I have read in current philosophical journals, I doubt if I can recall twenty discussions of even near-theological topics. The days seem long ago when Gladstone was debating detailed theological points with T. H. Huxley in one of the leading London monthly reviews. In fact they were still debating them only ten years before I was born. We have forcibly to remind ourselves that there had been an enormously long period during which most of the major theoretical issues had arisen out of disputes between one theology and another, or between theology and science, or history or morality or ordinary good sense. When theological coals were hot, the kettle of theological philosophy boiled briskly. If the kettle of theological philosophy is now not even steaming, it is because that fire has died down. Kettles cannot keep themselves on the boil. A philosopher cannot invent conceptual stresses and strains. He has to feel them if he is to be irked into dealing with them.

I do not want to exaggerate. The theological fire has died down, but it has not quite gone out and the kettle of theological philosophy, though far from even simmering, is not quite stone cold. Some philosophers, some of the time, do take some interest in tensions between theological, scientific and moral ideas. Others are at least polemically interested enough to deny that theological dictions convey any ideas at all. But most of us, most of the time, do just forget about the subject. Indeed we are not very often or very cogently reminded of it. Notice that what I am talking about is not religion but theology — an academic subject which has its rival schools, its professors, its dissertations, its journals, its examinations and its degrees and has its orthodoxies and its heresies too.

So while we ought to realize how untheological our interests have recently become, we need not, I think, feel professionally apologetic about it.

A. Q. Another traditional department of academic philosophy that has suffered some neglect in recent years is the philosophical study of politics. An important and perhaps the most widely influential aspect of British Hegelianism, it seems to have been borne down in the general collapse of that way of doing philosophy. I should not want to see it resurrected in its old form, with genuine philosophical problems and discussions inextricably embedded in a mass of alien matter, mixed up with history, theoretical political science, recommendations of policies, the comparative study of institutions and so on. There is no point in trying to do half a dozen things at once. In fact I think that this undifferentiating omnicompetence aspired to by traditional political theory has had an unfortunate effect on the scientific study of politics in this country. In the guise of commonsensical description and comparison of political institutions it has come to be little more than a modest and self-effacing appendage to history: following the Bagehot who wrote *The English Constitution* but oblivious of the Bagehot who wrote *Physics and Politics*.

So for this reason I should like to see more attention given to the philosophical problems raised by the scientific study of human society — problems posed by the complexity of the subject-matter, by the fact that the observer is part of what he observes and that his theories will influence the domain to which they refer, by the supposed uniqueness of situations in which human beings are involved, by the limited applicability to human society of experimental and quantitative methods and so on. This subject has a bad name but the recent interest in critical, rather than speculative, philosophy of history, in the philosophical study of the historian's procedure, may encourage an extension of the same approach to the less well-established ways of studying human affairs.

And, as a matter of fact, the genuinely philosophical part of the traditional corpus of political theory is by no means neglected. A revival of interest can be expected here from the new developments in a closely related field, which shares many problems — problems about rights and sovereignty, for example — with it, I mean the philosophy of law. Here justice is at last being done to the tradition of British analytical jurisprudence that stems from Bentham and Austin.

It seems to me, then, that the work that is already being done, and which will, one hopes, increase on problems of a conceptual or methodological order arising in law, history and the social sciences provides some answer to the charge that our preoccupations are trivial, academic or unreal.

M. W. The kind of subjects you have been discussing are, of course, closely connected with moral philosophy and here again I don't think the charge of triviality is wholly justified. Sometimes I suspect that people assume that all philosophy, and especially moral philosophy, has become frivolous just because they miss a certain tone of voice, a certain sonority of style which they connect with proper philosophy, philosophy as it ought to be done. People are uneasy because, for example, trivial or ludicrous examples are discussed instead of realistic or serious cases. But this doesn't, I think, constitute a very profound criticism of the present state of the subject. After all, you can extract something serious and interesting from the most trivial example provided that the example is well-chosen and clear. And advances in a subject are just as likely to go with clarity of style as with heaviness and obscurity. Still, there may well be a more serious discontent with moral philosophy which would be better worth taking into account. I mean the kind of criticism of current views which Miss Murdoch suggested in her essay on Metaphysics and Ethics. It may well be that many contemporary moral philosophers in England are too rigidly tied to certain unquestioned assumptions, of a mainly liberal and protestant kind, and that this, as Miss Murdoch suggests, unduly narrows their interests and makes it impossible for them to penetrate the complexities of the subject very deeply. It is no doubt true that we should do better to explore other people's different assumptions further, and if necessary to invent new concepts to help us in our analyses of human behaviour. At least we should do better if we didn't confine ourselves to such broad and well-worn concepts as 'goodness', 'duty' and 'ought'. But, although it is valuable to have this kind of criticism brought to our attention, it still needs to be remembered that however resolutely we widen our horizons, we shall not be able to go back to the kind of ethical theory which was supposed to derive from some total explanation of man's place in the universe. This does not mean, of course, that we cannot learn from metaphysicians; it seems to me, for instance, that there is much to be learned from Spinoza, even by one who would reject his system as a whole. But I don't think that incorporating new concepts into moral philosophy will have any very radical effects. It may well make the subject more interesting, but it will not change its character altogether.

G. R. What, to wind everything up, has been going on during our discussions?

Well, we have not arrived at a passable dictionary definition of 'metaphysics'. But we have agreed pretty well which philosophers should wear the label 'metaphysician'.

We have also agreed pretty well in our appreciation of the things that the big metaphysicians of the past did. First, they ontologized; that is, they essayed to prove assertions of existence from conceptual considerations. This was a mistake. Secondly, they tried, as we try, to trace and relieve logical stresses between the organizing ideas of everyday and technical thinking; and from their work in these fields we have valuable lessons to learn. Third, they set many examples of philosophizing which we are often scolded, sometimes justly and sometimes unjustly, for refusing to follow. We, it is said, shirk giving concrete guidance; we do not preach; we are untheological; we are excessively microscopic; we neglect political problems; our moral philosophy is too thin; and in general, we stick too closely to the grindstone and go too little out into the woods.

I hope that these good marks that we have given, and these bad marks that we have received in return, will keep us all modest enough to go on learning.

THE END

PRINTED BY R. & R. CLARK, LTD., EDINBURGH